Blessed in the Darkness

How All Things Are Working for Your Good

Joel Osteen

Faith
Words

LARGE PRINT

ALSO BY JOEL OSTEEN

Blessed in the Darkness Study Guide
Break Out!
Break Out! Journal
Daily Readings from Break Out!
Every Day a Friday
Every Day a Friday Journal
Daily Readings from Every Day a Friday
Fresh Start
Fresh Start Study Guide
I Declare
I Declare Personal Application Guide
The Power of I Am
The Power of I Am Journal
The Power of I Am Study Guide
Daily Readings from The Power of I Am
Think Better, Live Better
Think Better, Live Better Journal
Think Better, Live Better Study Guide
Daily Readings from Think Better, Live Better
Wake Up to Hope Devotional
(with Victoria Osteen)
You Can, You Will
You Can, You Will Journal
Daily Readings from You Can, You Will
Your Best Life Now
Scriptures and Meditations for Your Best Life Now
Daily Readings from Your Best Life Now
Your Best Life Begins Each Morning
Your Best Life Now Study Guide
Your Best Life Now for Moms
Your Best Life Now Journal
Starting Your Best Life Now

FaithWords

LARGE PRINT

FaithWords
Hachette Book Group
1290 Avenue of the Americas, New York, NY 10104
faithwords.com
twitter.com/faithwords

First Edition: October 2017

FaithWords is a division of Hachette Book Group, Inc. The FaithWords name and logo are trademarks of Hachette Book Group, Inc.

The publisher is not responsible for websites (or their content) that are not owned by the publisher.

The Hachette Speakers Bureau provides a wide range of authors for speaking events. To find out more, go to www.hachettespeakersbureau.com or call (866) 376-6591.

Literary development: Lance Wubbels Literary Services, Bloomington, Minnesota.

Library of Congress Cataloging-in-Publication Data

Names: Osteen, Joel, author.
Title: Blessed in the darkness / Joel Osteen.
Description: New York : FaithWords, [2017]
Identifiers: LCCN 2017020080| ISBN 9781455534326 (hardcover) |
    ISBN 9781478923947 (large print) | ISBN 9781478991816 (Spanish edition) |
    ISBN 9781478987185 (audio download) | ISBN 9781478987123 (audio book) |
    ISBN 9781455534319 (ebook)
Subjects: LCSH: Consolation. | Suffering—Religious aspects—Christianity. |
    Providence and government of God—Christianity.
Classification: LCC BV4905.3 .O88 2017 | DDC 248.8/6—dc23
LC record available at https://lccn.loc.gov/2017020080

ISBN: 978-1-4555-3432-6 (hardcover), 978-1-4555-3431-9 (ebook),
978-1-4789-2394-7 (large print), 978-1-5460-2713-3 (signed edition),
978-1-5460-2412-6 (B&N signed edition), 978-1-5460-3317-2 (international
trade paperback), 978-1-5460-3177-2 (South African trade)

Printed in the United States of America

LSC-C

10 9 8 7 6 5 4 3 2 1

CONTENTS

Blessed in the Darkness

CHAPTER ONE

Blessed in the Dark Places

When we think about what it means to be "blessed," most of the time we think of the good things that have happened to us. Perhaps our supervisor offered us a new position at work, and we were blessed with a promotion. We remember when our new baby was born, and how we were blessed with a child. Or we may have overcome an illness and been blessed with a return to good health. Blessings and good times go hand in hand. It's easy to celebrate and have a grateful attitude when things are going our way.

But what about when we go through really difficult times? The company was downsizing, and we were laid off. Somebody walked out of a relationship with us, and now we have to start all over. Where are the blessings when we go through things we don't understand?

I met a young lady who had been pregnant for five months with her first child. She had been so excited that she had already decorated the baby's room, but something went wrong with the pregnancy, and she had a miscarriage. She was numb with grief, expressionless, in a dark place.

In 1981 my family thought we'd be celebrating the Christmas holidays together, enjoying fun and fellowship. Instead we learned that my mother had been diagnosed with terminal liver cancer and given a few weeks to live. It was a very somber Christmas. Is it possible that we can gain blessings in these times of darkness that we cannot gain in the light?

All of us at some point will go through a dark place—a sickness, a divorce, a loss, a child who breaks our heart. It's easy to get discouraged, give up on our dreams, and think that's the end. But God uses the dark places. They're a part of His divine plan. Think of a seed. As long as a seed remains in the light, it cannot germinate and will never become what it was created to be. The seed must be planted in the soil, in a dark place, so that the potential on the inside will come to life.

There are seeds of greatness in us—dreams, goals, talents, potential— that will only come to life in a dark place.

In the same way, there are seeds of greatness in us—dreams, goals, talents, potential—that will only come to life in a dark place.

The Dark Places Bring Us Blessings

Throughout the Scripture, every person who did something great went through one of these dark places. Moses made a mistake and killed an Egyptian man. He spent forty lonely years on the back side of the desert, feeling as though he had blown it. But in that dark place something was

> *The dark place was a prerequisite for his stepping into the fullness of his destiny.*

being shaped in his life. He was being prepared, developing patience, humility, strength, and trust. Without the dark place Moses would never have held up his rod and parted the Red Sea. He would never have led the Israelites out of slavery and toward the Promised Land. The dark place was a prerequisite for his stepping into the fullness of his destiny, and it's a prerequisite for us as well.

Esther was an orphan, having lost both of her parents, and living in a foreign country. She felt alone, forsaken, abandoned, in a dark place. Yet God used her to help save the people of Israel. Joseph was betrayed by his own brothers, falsely accused of a crime, and put in prison, a dark place. But he ended up ruling a nation. Elijah descended from a great mountain victory into a dark place of depression so low that he wanted to die, yet he's one of the heroes of faith. David had an affair with a married woman, and then he had her husband killed in battle. But after an extremely dark time that followed in his life, David turned his heart back to the Lord and is remembered as "the man after God's heart."

You may not realize it, but it's in the dark places that you really grow. They're where your character is developed, where you learn to trust God and to persevere, and where your spiritual muscles are made strong. In the dark places you pray more, you draw closer to God, and you take time to get quiet and listen to what He's saying. In those dark places you reevaluate your priorities, you slow down and take time for family, and you get a new appreciation for what God has given you.

A friend of mine was given the devastating news that because of an infection he was going to lose his eyesight. He had surgery and wasn't supposed to be able to see afterward. But the doctors were able to correct the problem. Amazingly, he came out of the surgery with his vision perfectly fine. Now every morning when he gets up, he takes fifteen minutes and just stares at the trees and the flowers, and he gazes in wonder at his children. He didn't realize it at the time, but in that dark place he was being blessed. Something was happening on the inside. He was experiencing new growth, a greater confidence, endurance, and resolve.

Iron Will Enter Your Soul

When you go through enough dark places, you don't complain about life's little inconveniences. You don't get upset because you didn't get a parking spot. You don't lose your joy when you get stuck in traffic. You don't get offended if a coworker was rude to you. You've been through too much to let that sour you. Your backbone has been made into steel.

One day a well-meaning person said to me, "Joel, I heard a guy talking negatively about you, and I was so sorry he said that." The person was being kind and encouraging. But I thought to myself, *You don't have to feel sorry for me. I buried my father. I saw my mother come through cancer. I learned how to minister when every voice told me I couldn't do it. I believed we could get the Compaq Center when all the odds were against us. If I made it through all that, I can make it through somebody not liking me.* That's like a little gnat that you just have to flick away.

When you go through a few dark places, it toughens you up. The dark places are what have made me into who I am today. I like the good times better. I prefer everything going my way. I'm not believing for any dark times, but it wasn't the good times that brought out the best in me. It was the lonely nights, the times I didn't think I could do it on my own, the times I didn't see a way—that's when I learned how to really pray, that's when I developed an unshakable confidence in God, that's when my faith was stretched. Don't complain about the dark times; there's a blessing in the dark places. God is working something in your life that can only be worked in the fire of affliction.

When my father died and I was first trying to learn how to minister, I was so afraid to get up in front of people. There were nights after dinner when I would go to my closet to pray. Victoria would come looking for me, asking the kids, "Where's your dad?" She would find me in my closet praying. The truth is, I never prayed like that in the good times. I didn't go out of my way to draw closer to God when everything was going my way. It was the dark places that helped me to develop my spiritual muscles. Even though I didn't like what I was going through, being so uncomfortable forced me to stretch and grow. I wouldn't change it for anything. It's made me better.

God uses the dark places. When Joseph was falsely accused and put in prison for thirteen years, the Scripture says, "He was laid in chains of iron, and his soul entered into that iron." In that prison Joseph developed strength, a perseverance that he could not have gotten any other way. There are some lessons you can only learn in the dark places. Quit complaining about what you're going through, about how unfair it is, about who did you wrong. It may be uncomfortable, you may not like it, but it's working for your good. You're getting stronger; it's developing something in you that you can only get in the dark. You can't reach your highest potential being in the light all the time. To have no opposition, no problems, and nobody coming against you may sound good, but it will stunt your growth.

> *"He was laid in chains of iron, and his soul entered into that iron."*

Enlarged in Times of Distress

King David said, "God enlarged me in my time of distress." He didn't get enlarged in the good times; he was enlarged when things weren't going

his way. As a teenager he wanted to be out having fun with friends, but he got stuck taking
care of his father's sheep. Day after day, while he
was out there alone in the shepherds' fields with
nobody to talk to, it looked as though he would
never accomplish his dreams. But those years in
the lonely fields were what helped prepare him to
become a champion. When he killed Goliath, the
people called him an overnight success. But the
truth is, it didn't happen overnight. It happened
because he went through the dark places with a
good attitude. When he wasn't getting his way,
when he was lonely and felt as though God had
forgotten about him, he just kept doing the right
thing. He understood this principle. His attitude
was, *God, this is a dark place. I may not see it
now, but I believe it's working for me. I'm getting
stronger. I'm developing patience and perseverance
and learning to trust You.* At the right time he not
only came out of that dark place, but came out
increased, promoted, and better off than he had
been before.

It's not a coincidence that David says in Psalm
23, "The Lord is my shepherd; I shall not want.
He makes me to lie down in green pastures; He
leads me beside the still waters....And though I
walk through the valley of the shadow of death,

I will fear no evil." He was saying, in effect, *The same God who leads me to the green pastures, the same God who leads me to the still waters, is the same God who will lead me through the valley of the shadow of death.*

We can all trust God when we're resting in the green pastures, and we can trust Him when we're beside the still waters—that's easy. But He is asking you to trust Him when you're in the dark valley. He hasn't left you. You may feel alone, abandoned, and mistreated, and think that life hasn't been fair, but God is still leading you. That dark place is a part of the plan to make you into who you were created to be. It may not be easy, you may not understand it, but faith is trusting in God when life doesn't make sense. Dare to believe that He's blessing you even in the dark places. Believe that what's meant for your harm is going to work to your advantage.

David went on to say, "After you go through the dark place in the valley, God will anoint your head with oil, He'll prepare a table before you in the presence of your enemies, and your cup will run over." Notice that you have to go through the valley to enjoy the table set before you. You have to go through the loneliness, through the sickness, through the betrayal before you get that fresh anointing, that new beginning. You have to go through the shepherds' fields, doing the right thing when the wrong thing is happening. You have to go through the job where you're not being treated right, through the struggle, the lack, the debt, before you make it to where your cup runs over.

Too often we want the overflow but not the valley. Our prayer is, "God, give me more favor, more influence, a greater anointing." God says, "Okay, but you have to be willing to go with Me through the valley." In the dark places is where we prove to God what we're really made of. Can God trust you with more of His favor, with greater influence and more resources? You have to be faithful in the shepherds' field, where it's lonely and where you're not getting your way. "Well, Joel, I don't like my boss. That's why I slack off at work, and that's why I come in late. They don't treat me right." If you don't have a good attitude in the dark places, you'll get stuck there. If you're not faithful in the wilderness, how can God trust you to be faithful in the Promised Land?

> *Too often we want the overflow but not the valley.*

Question Marks Changed to Exclamation Points

Have a new perspective: the dark places are opportunities to grow. You're not in a dark place by accident. If God weren't going to use it for your good, He wouldn't have allowed it. You may not understand it, it may not make sense, but God knows what He's doing. Pass the test.

When my father went to be with the Lord in 1999, that was the greatest challenge I had ever faced—a dark place. When you go through a loss, it's easy to get discouraged and feel as though God let you down and there will never be any more good days. But I've learned that every time something dies in my life, something else is coming to life. It looks like an end, but God has a new beginning. A friend betrays you and walks away, and your relationship dies, but at the same time God is birthing a new relationship. He's already lined up another friend who is destined to cross your path. You lost a job, a position, or a major client, but God has a new position, new opportunities, and new levels for you. If you'll go through the valley trusting, believing, knowing that God is in control, you'll come to the table prepared for you, into the fresh anointing, and increase to where your cup is running over.

I have a friend I played baseball with years ago. He was the star player, always the best one on the field. He led the league in hitting and fielding. His dream was to play professional baseball. During one summer he was invited to play on a highly competitive amateur team that traveled around the country. Only extremely talented players got the opportunity to play on this very prestigious team. He played that summer and did exceptionally well, but some of the other players were jealous of him. They began to spread lies about him and stir up trouble. The next year the coach, even though he liked my friend very much, believed the rumors and didn't invite him back to play. My friend was very discouraged. He tried to get on several other teams, but it was too late. They were already full. For the first time he didn't have a summer team to play on. He missed the whole season—no games, no opportunities, a dark place. He didn't understand it, and it wasn't fair, but he didn't get bitter. He knew the same God Who had led him to the quiet waters and green pastures was leading him through the valley.

Every night he would go to the batting cages and keep improving his skills. He'd have friends hit him balls so he could stay sharp in his fielding. He kept lifting weights, running, staying in shape. He had no team to play for, and he had not been treated right, but he knew that on the other side of the valley was the table already prepared for him. You have to go through the valley to get to the table. Don't get stuck in the dark valley. Don't lose your passion and have a sour attitude that says, "I don't understand why this happened. After all these years, they laid me off." "How could I get this bad medical report?" "Why did this person break my heart?" If you're always trying to figure out why, you're going to get stuck.

Think about this: an exclamation point is simply a question mark straightened out. If you want God to turn your question marks, the things you don't understand, into exclamation points, you have to trust Him. In those dark places where it isn't fair, instead of wondering why something happened, dare to say, "God, I know You're still on the throne. I may not understand this valley I'm in, but I know that on the other side is my exclamation point. The table is already prepared, the right people are waiting, a fresh anointing is coming with increase, promotion, and a new level." If you go through the dark places like that, you'll see that question mark turned into an exclamation point. God will amaze you with His goodness.

That's what happened to us. When my father

> *If you go through the dark places like that, you'll see that question mark turned into an exclamation point.*

died, I had a lot of question marks. "Will the church make it? Can I really minister? Will anyone listen to me?" As I stayed in faith and went through the dark places with the right attitude, one by one God turned the question marks into exclamation points. "Will the church make it?" Yes, and here's a Compaq Center to hold all the people—exclamation point. "Can I really minister? Will anyone listen to me?" Yes, and here are some TV networks that will carry your program, here are some number one books, and here is a SiriusXM satellite radio channel—exclamation point.

Blessings through Breakings

You may be in a dark place right now. You went through a breakup, and you're hurt, lonely, wondering if you'll ever be happy again. I can tell you firsthand—I'm a living witness—that if you'll keep moving forward, honoring God, He'll bring somebody into your life who is better than you ever imagined—somebody kinder, friendlier, more loving, who'll treat you like a king, a queen. The latter part of your life will be better than the first part. God has an exclamation point waiting for you.

Maybe you're dealing with a sickness. You've been told that it doesn't look good. Stay in faith—

the exclamation point is coming. My mother was diagnosed with terminal cancer, and thirty-six years later, she's still healthy and strong. That's good, but here's the exclamation point. Every week she goes to the hospital to pray for other sick people. That's God making the enemy pay.

Perhaps you're in a dark place in your finances. You had a setback or lost a client, and you're wondering, *Is it ever going to get better?* Yes, on the other side of that valley you're going to find your cup that runs over—increase, abundance, a new level of your destiny. You may have been in that valley for a long time, but you need to get ready. You're about to see the breakthrough, and the problem is about to turn around. Don't stop believing. Get your fire back, because God did not bring you this far to leave you. He has an exclamation point coming your way.

That's what happened to my friend the baseball player. One day he was out practicing, minding his own business and improving his skills. What he didn't know was that there was a scout for a professional team up in the stands. This scout was there to watch another player. But when he saw how talented my friend was, he called him over and said, "I'd like you to come try out for our team." That was God putting him at the right place at the right time. God knows how to get you to your destiny. My friend went and tried out. He made the team, played a few years in the minor leagues, kept moving up, and went on to play in the big leagues. He had a long, successful career.

People don't determine your destiny, but God does. A bad break can't stop you, sickness can't stop you, injustice can't stop you. God has the final say. If you'll go through the dark places with a good attitude and keep doing the right thing, you will come into your exclamation point. You will see the goodness of God.

When Jesus was about to feed a multitude of thousands of people, He had a little boy's lunch, just five loaves of bread and two fish. He held the loaves up and gave thanks, and then, the Scripture says, "He broke the loaves," and the bread was multiplied. Notice the blessing was in the breaking. The more He broke it, the more it multiplied.

There are times in life when we feel broken: we have broken dreams, a broken heart. When the young lady told me that she had had a miscarriage, big tears ran down her beautiful face. She said, "This baby is what I wanted more than anything else." She was broken. When I lost my father, I felt as though a part of me had died. When you feel broken, don't get bitter, don't give up on your dreams. That brokenness is not the end; it's a sign that God is about to multiply. That's what David said: "God enlarged me in my time of distress." That brokenness may have been meant to stop you, but if you'll stay in faith, God is going to use it to increase you. The loss, the disappointment, the person who didn't keep their word—you feel the hurt, but the truth is that these were setting you up for God to increase you.

If you have gone through more than your share of bad breaks, take heart. The more broken you are, the more God is going to increase you. The bigger the disappointment, the bigger the blessing. The more they hurt you, the more He's going to reward you. He has beauty for your ashes, joy for your mourning. The brokenness is only

The bigger the disappointment, the bigger the blessing.

temporary. Don't settle in the valley, don't even get comfortable in the valley, for the valley is not your home. The Shepherd is leading you through the valley. On the other side is abundance, fullness of joy, great relationships, health and wholeness, and dreams coming to pass.

Bring Out the Greatness on the Inside

Jesus said, "Unless a kernel of wheat is planted in the soil and dies, it remains alone. But if it dies, it will produce much fruit." You can have a seed on your desk for a lifetime, but it will never become what it was created to be until you put it in the ground. Its potential will never be released until it's been planted. As long as it's on the desk where it's comfortable and it doesn't have to stretch or deal with any adversity, the seed's potential will stay locked up on the inside. Only after it's planted and goes through the process of germination—when the outer shell breaks off and the new growth begins—will it blossom and bring forth much fruit. The problem with many people is that they want the fruit, but they don't want to go through the process. They don't want to be uncomfortable. They don't want to have to stretch or deal with adversity, opposition, or betrayal. But without the dark place, your potential will stay locked on the inside. The seed cannot germinate in the light.

If you were to ask the seed, I'm sure it would say, "I don't want to go into the dirt. It's dark, it's lonely, and it's uncomfortable when people walk on top of me." The seed feels as though it's been buried, as though it's the end, but what the seed doesn't realize is that it's not buried; it's planted. It has the life of Almighty God on the inside. That dark place, even though it's uncomfortable, is a critical part of the process. Over a period of time, once it germinates and grows, instead of being one little buried seed, it ends up being a beautiful flower, blossoming and bearing much fruit. If you were to ask the flower when it was fully in blossom, it would say, "I didn't like the dark place, but I realize now it was a blessing. Look what it brought out of me. Look what I've become!"

There will be times in life when it feels as though you're buried, and thoughts will tell you, *You've seen your best days. That layoff ruined your career. That divorce tainted your future. This sickness is going to be the end of you.* Have a new perspective.

You're not buried; you're planted.

You're not buried; you're planted. If you never went through the dark place—the loneliness, the disappointment, the loss—you would never discover what's on the inside. Like that seed's, your potential is about to be released. You're not only going to come out of the darkness, you're going to come out better, stronger, fully in blossom, and bearing much fruit. When you feel as if something is dying, it's dark, you feel the pressure of the dirt, you don't see a way out, that's a sign that something new is about to come to life—new growth, new talent, new opportunities.

When my father went to be with the Lord, I felt as though I were buried. I could feel the pressure, but in that dark time, when something was dying, God was birthing something new. That's when I discovered gifts and talents that I hadn't known I had. I didn't like the process, but that's what caused me to blossom. None of us like to be planted; it's uncomfortable, it's lonely, but in those dark places you have to remind yourself that new growth is on the way. Even though it feels as if something is dying, something else is coming to life. You're not buried; you're planted. When you come out, you're going to bear much fruit.

My challenge is for you to be willing to go through the process. Too many people get bitter, lose their passion, and get stuck with the unanswered question, "Why is this happening? I thought God was for me." Dare to trust Him. He knows what He's doing. He doesn't send the difficulty, but He will use it. Don't fight the dark places. There may be dirt all around you, it's uncomfortable, but that dirt is not there to stop you. It's there to bring out the greatness on the inside. If you'll go through the dark places with a good attitude, God is going to take your question marks and turn them into exclamation points. You will go through every valley and find a table that's already set for you, a fresh anointing, and you'll increase to where your cup runs over. You're not buried; you're planted. It's just a matter of time before you break out and blossom into who you were created to be.

CHAPTER TWO

Night Seasons

There are times in all our lives when things are not changing as fast as we would like. We're praying and believing, but our health isn't improving. Our finances haven't turned around. We still haven't met the right person. We can feel alone, forgotten, as though our situation is never going to change. It's a night season. In these night seasons, we can't see what God is doing. It doesn't look as though anything is happening, but God is working behind the scenes. He does His greatest work in the dark. We don't see anything changing. We're still dealing with the same problem. But God hasn't forgotten about us.

In the dark times, when life feels unfair, you have to remind yourself that God is still in control. Just because you don't see anything happening doesn't mean that God is not working. He doesn't always show you what He's up to. It's easy to trust Him when you're getting good breaks and things are going great. But you have to learn to trust Him in the night seasons when things aren't going your way and you don't see anything happening.

As a young man, David defeated Goliath. It was a great victory. But after that he spent years running from King Saul, hiding in caves, sleeping in the desert. I'm sure he prayed, "God, deliver me from Saul. This is not right." But it was as though the heavens were silent. God didn't change it. Saul was wrong. It was unfair to David. But the night seasons are times of testing, times of proving.

The night seasons are times of testing, times of proving.

We can either choose to get negative and live discouraged, or we can choose to say, "God, I don't understand it. It's not fair, but I trust in You. I know You're not just the God of the daytime, but also the God of the night seasons."

In the Scripture, Ruth lost her husband at an early age. She was devastated, heartbroken. She could have given up on life and lived in self-pity. But she understood this principle: the night seasons are not the end. The bad breaks, the disappointments, the losses, and the sicknesses are simply additional steps on the way to your destiny.

The psalmist said, "Weeping may endure for a night, but joy comes in the morning." Your story doesn't end in the night. The night is temporary. The sickness is temporary. The loneliness is temporary. The addiction is temporary. Ruth went on to meet another man. They fell in love, got married, and had a baby. Her story didn't end in the dark. When things aren't working out and you feel as though you're going in the wrong direction, don't get discouraged because God has not changed it yet. It's just a night season. It's not permanent. It's not how your story ends. You may not see anything happening, but God is at work. Dare to trust Him. Keep moving forward in faith, keep believing. It's just a matter of time before the morning breaks forth.

"After This"

Like other Old Testament heroes of the faith, Job went through a night season. Everything had been going great. He was happy, healthy, and successful, but life took a sudden turn. Out of nowhere he came down with a very painful illness. He had boils all over his body. He lost his business, and he lost his sons and daughters. His whole world was turned upside down. What's interesting is that

Job was a good man. He loved God. He was a person of excellence and integrity. All that happened to him would make more sense if he were a compromiser, making wrong choices, not honoring God. But the Scripture says, "God sends the rain on the just and the unjust." Just because you're a good person doesn't mean you're not going to have some night seasons.

If you are in a difficult time right now, it doesn't mean you've done something wrong and that God's not pleased with you, that you don't have His favor. It means that you're getting some rain. Without the rain you couldn't grow. And God wouldn't have allowed it if it were going to keep you from your destiny. He has you in the palms of His hands. He's closely watching you. You may feel as though you're in the fire, but God controls the thermostat. He won't let it be more than you can handle. Now quit telling yourself, "I'll never make it through this. I'll never get well, never accomplish my dreams." No, it's just a night season. It's not a surprise to God. He already has the solution, and the breakthrough is headed your way.

But Job did what many of us do in the difficult times. He focused on the problem, magnified what was wrong, and let it overwhelm him. Job said, "I will never again experience pleasure. I have been assigned to long weary nights of misery." He was saying, "This is permanent. This is how my story ends. I've been assigned to nights of misery." The events our ministry calls "A Night of Hope" Job would have called "A Night of Misery." I'm not making light of

Job did what many of us do in the difficult times. He focused on the problem, magnified what was wrong, and let it overwhelm him.

what he faced, because it was serious and heart-breaking. But the mistake he made was thinking it was permanent.

What you're going through may be difficult, but the good news is that you are going through it. It's not your final destination. It's a night season, not a night lifetime. In Job's darkest hour, when he was the most discouraged, one of his friends said to him, "God will fill your mouth with laughter, and your lips with shouts of joy." God was saying, "Job, it looks bad. You don't understand it, but don't worry. It's not permanent. It's just a season. I'm about to fill your mouth with laughter."

God is saying to you what He said to Job. Life may not have been fair, but you're not going to live discouraged, overwhelmed by problems or burdened down by illnesses. Joy is coming. Health is coming. Breakthroughs are coming. Promotion is coming. God is about to fill your mouth with laughter. That means God's going to do something so unusual, so extraordinary, that you'll be so amazed that all you can do is laugh. Your mourning is going to be turned to dancing, your sorrow to joy.

This is what happened with Job. He not only made it through the night season, but God restored double what he'd lost. He came out with twice the oxen, sheep, camels, and donkeys. He felt twice as healthy. God always makes the enemy pay for bringing trouble. If you'll stay in faith, you won't just come out, you will come out better than you were before. The Scripture says, "After this, Job lived 140 years, and saw his children and grandchildren for four generations. Then he died an old man, having lived a long, good life." When we think of Job, we usually think of all his pain, all his suffering. The truth is, that was just one season. You may be in a dark time, but, like Job, you're going to come through it and still live a long, blessed life. It says, "After this, Job lived 140 years." After what? After the night season. That means after the loss, after the disappointment, after the divorce, after the sickness, there are still many great days ahead.

Light Will Come Bursting In

My father went through a night season. He was married at a very young age. Unfortunately, the marriage didn't work out. He was devastated when it failed, resigned from his church, and got out of the ministry. Denominational leaders told him that he would never pastor again. People said he was finished. The good news is, people don't determine your destiny; God does. Two years later, he got back into the ministry, and he later married my mother. They had five children and were married for almost fifty years. They started Lakewood and he pastored here for forty years, touching the world. This all happened after the divorce, after the disappointment. He'd thought that would sour the rest of his life, but it was just a season. He went on to live a long, blessed, faith-filled life. Don't let the night seasons convince you that you've seen your best days. You wouldn't be alive unless God had something amazing in front of you.

In the dark times, it's easy to talk about the difficulties, talk about how badly life is treating us. Like Job, we tend to exaggerate our problems. All that's going to do is make you more discouraged and defeated and take your joy. Instead of complaining, one of the best things you can say is, "All is well." When you say, "All is well," what you're really saying is,

> *In the dark times, it's easy to talk about the difficulties, talk about how badly life is treating us.*

"God is still on the throne, and I'm not going to live upset, bitter, and guilty. I may be in a night season, but I know this too shall pass. All is well." Somebody may say, "Well, I thought the medical report wasn't good." And you respond, "Yes, that's true, but all is well. God is restoring health back to me." They say, "Your child is still off course." You answer, "Yes, but I'm not worried. All is well. As for me and my house, we will serve the Lord."

Perhaps you're wondering, *How can I say "All is well" when I lost a loved one, and I went through a breakup and still haven't met the right person?* You can say it because you know the night season is only temporary. You know joy is coming. You know that what was meant for harm, God is turning to your advantage. You know that after this comes a long, blessed, faith-filled life. Now, don't talk yourself into being miserable. We all have night seasons, times we don't understand. Keep a report of victory coming out of your mouth. If you're going to magnify something, don't magnify your problems; magnify your God. Talk about His greatness, talk about His favor. And yes, you may have big challenges, but we serve a big God. A cure may seem impossible, but God can do the impossible. An obstacle may look permanent, but one touch of God's favor can thrust you to the next level. Quit worrying. God is saying, "All is well." In your finances, all is well. In your health, all is well. In your family, all is well. It may be night right now, but morning is coming. You're going to see what God was doing behind the scenes.

Every day that you stay in faith, every day that you keep a good attitude despite the darkness, you're passing the test. That night season will come to an end. The psalmist said, "When darkness overtakes the righteous, light will come bursting in." It's going to happen suddenly, unexpectedly; you won't see it coming. You woke up, and it was still dark. Nothing had changed, but suddenly you get the break you need. Suddenly your health turns around. Suddenly you meet the right person. The light comes bursting in.

The Development of Character

Maybe, as we saw Moses did in the first chapter, you made a mistake that put you into a night season. Something was delayed. You had to take a detour to a desert place. You're not where you thought you would be. Now you think you have to settle there and never accomplish what God put in your heart. You

> *In that night season, Moses changed. He learned to wait on God, to listen to His voice, to walk in humility.*

may not realize it, but right now, God is getting you prepared for your comeback. What He started, He's going to finish. He's already taken into account every wrong turn, every mistake, every bad break in your life. It may look like the end to you, but the truth is, it's just a temporary delay. It's a time of testing, a time of proving, when your character is being developed. God is working in you, polishing off the rough edges. He's getting you prepared for where He's taking you. Forty years after Moses' mistake, God came back and said, "All right, Moses, now you're ready for Me to use you to deliver My people." The Scripture says, "Moses was the most humble man in all the land." In that night season, Moses changed. He learned to wait on God, to listen to His voice, to walk in humility. He came up higher in his character.

In the difficult times, stay pliable, stay open, and say, "God, make me and mold me. Show me where I need to change." You grow in the tough times. Even physically, you grow at night when you're asleep. In the same way, when you're in a night season, you may not like it, but it's working for you. You're getting stronger. You have to be prepared for where God is taking you. Moses couldn't handle it the first time. He made a mistake and had to run, but God didn't write him off. He didn't cancel Moses' destiny. He used the night season to refine him.

When Saul was chasing David through the desert, there were several opportunities for David to kill Saul. He could have taken Saul's life and gotten rid of his problem, so to speak. But David wouldn't do it. He knew that Saul had been anointed by God. He told his men, "I'm not going to harm what God has anointed." After he passed these tests, after David showed God what he was made of, that he was a man of character and integrity, God took care of Saul and David was made the king.

In the night seasons, you need to pass the tests, change where you need to change, and deal with the areas that God is bringing to light. You need to prove to Him that you'll do the right thing when it's hard, and you'll forgive others even though they hurt you. Then, as He did for David and Moses, because your character has been developed, God will bring you out of that night season and get you to where you're supposed to be. But we can only develop some things in the dark. Without the night seasons, we wouldn't become all God created us to be.

Transformed in the Dark

A caterpillar can be going along just fine. Everything is great, but down deep something says, "You're not supposed to crawl your whole life. You have more in you." He gets excited, thinking, *Yes, that's right!* Then he looks in the mirror and says, "What was I thinking? I'll never fly. I'm just a glorified worm. That's impossible." But one day the caterpillar spins a cocoon around itself and hangs upside down from a branch. It's dark. He can't move or eat. If you were to talk to him when he is in the cocoon, he would say, "Let me go back to where I was. Let me go back to being a caterpillar. I don't like where I am. I'm uncomfortable. It's dark. It's lonely." What he doesn't realize is that in the dark, a transformation is taking place. Before long he starts feeling some wings, then he gets the strength to push out of that cocoon. Now, instead of crawling on the ground, he's a beautiful butterfly floating through the air.

Like the caterpillar, we all dislike the night seasons. We don't like being uncomfortable. We don't see anything happening. But there are times when God incubates us. He does not take us through the dark places to make us miserable, but in the dark a transformation is taking place. You're growing, you're being refined. You may not like it, but you have to keep reminding yourself that your wings are developing.

You're about to step up to a new level. No more crawling, living in mediocrity. You were made for higher things.

You're about to step up to a new level. No more crawling, living in mediocrity. You were made for higher things. You may be in a night season, but by faith I can see your cocoon starting to open. I see a wing coming out. This is no time to be discouraged; you're on the verge of taking off in flight. You're about to become a beautiful butterfly. You're about to go places that you've never dreamed of. Now, don't complain about the cocoon. "It's dark. It's uncomfortable. I'm lonely." Keep a good attitude; it's all a part of the process. God is changing you from glory to glory.

In the Scripture, a man named Jacob had not lived the right kind of life. He was dishonest. He cheated people and even tricked his brother out of his birthright. You would think that God wouldn't have anything to do with him. But God doesn't write us off. He keeps working with us and showing us His mercy as He did with Jacob. While Jacob was on a long journey through the desert, he was hot and tired and hungry. Nothing was going his way. He came to a place to spend the night, and all he could find for a pillow was a rock. He was in a hard place, a lonely time—a night season. I'm sure Jacob thought that God had forgotten about him. He went to sleep that night feeling down on himself, discouraged, full of regrets. While he was sleeping, he had a dream in which he saw the heavens open up, and saw a huge staircase with angels going up and down. The Lord was standing at the top of the staircase, and He said, "Jacob, the ground you are lying on belongs to you and your descendants. I will protect you wherever you go. I will be with you continually until I give you everything that I have promised." When Jacob woke up, he couldn't believe what he had seen. He said, "Surely the Lord is in this place!" What's interesting is that Jacob wasn't in a church, a temple, or a synagogue. He was in the desert. God was showing us that He's the God of hard places, the God of lonely times, the God of night seasons.

You may be in a difficult place now. Perhaps you're fighting a battle in your health, dealing with depression, or raising a special needs child. You feel alone, forgotten, and discouraged. God is right there with you, and, as they did for Jacob, I believe the heavens are about to open up. God is going to make things happen that you couldn't make happen. You may be in a hard place, but you're not staying there. Your health is going to improve. You're going to break that addiction. The right people are going to show up. You're going to join Jacob and say, "The Lord is in this place! The Lord healed me from cancer." "The Lord freed me from depression." "The Lord blessed my business." He's not going to stop until He's given you everything that He's promised.

Get Ready for Some *Wows*

You've heard the phrase *the night shift*. It refers to people who work during the night. But think of it another way. In the night, things are going to shift. The Scripture says, "God never sleeps." He doesn't just work the night shift, He shifts things in the night. You may be in a night season, and you may

Don't worry—a night shift is coming.

not see how the difficulties you face can work out. Don't worry—a night shift is coming. The God who works the night shift is going to shift things in your favor. There's going to be a shift in your health, a shift in your finances, a shift with that addiction. You think you're going to have it for years. It looks permanent. No, get ready for a night shift.

This is what happened with Paul and Silas. They had been spreading the good news in the city of Philippi, for which they had been beaten with rods and imprisoned, held in the inner dungeon with their feet in chains. But at midnight, as they were singing praises to God, suddenly there was a great earthquake. The prison doors flung open, and the chains came off their feet. They walked out as free men. What happened? God shifted the earth, shifted the prison doors, shifted the chains. When did it happen? At midnight. It was just another night shift for the God who works the night shift.

Things may look permanent in your life—the addiction, the sickness, the panic attacks, the lack and struggle. Thoughts will tell you, *You'll always have to deal with that.* Don't believe those lies. You're in a night season, which means you're in perfect position for a night shift. God specializes in shifting things in the dark. Instead of worrying, all through the day say, "Lord, thank You for a night shift. Thank You that things are changing in my favor. It's dark now, but I believe what You said. Light is about to come bursting in."

In Genesis 2, Adam was all by himself in the Garden of Eden. Life was good. He was naming the animals that God had created, enjoying the crystal-clear river, the beautiful trees, the delicious fruit. There were no problems, no sicknesses, no oppositions. Adam didn't think it could get any better. But God didn't want him to live alone. The Scripture says, "God caused Adam to fall into a deep sleep." God put him in a night season. He took a rib from his side and used it to create a woman. When Adam woke up from this deep sleep and saw Eve, I can imagine the first thing he said was, "Wow, God, You've outdone Yourself!" But I'm sure that he hadn't understood why God was putting him to sleep. He was happy already. Life seemed perfect. But some things can only develop in the dark. And if God didn't put us to sleep, so to speak—have us go through a night season—we would never see the fullness of what He has in store for us.

You may feel as though God has put you to sleep. Things have slowed down. You're in a challenging situation. It's a night season. Be encouraged. When you wake up and see what God has been up to, the first thing you're going to say is, "Wow, God, I never dreamed You'd take me here!" "I never dreamed we'd have the Compaq Center!" "I never dreamed I'd be this healthy again!" God has some *wows* in your future.

Don't complain about the dark places, because they are leading you to the amazing things God has in store. You may not understand it, but God wouldn't have allowed it if He weren't going to use it to your advantage. Right now, God is working behind the scenes. He sees what you're dealing with and knows how you feel. He's saying the night seasons are not permanent. You may be in a cocoon, where it's dark and uncomfortable, but

He's making you and molding you, your wings
are developing. You're about to take off in flight
to a new level. I believe you're about to see a
night shift from sickness to health, from lack to
abundance, from addiction to freedom. The light
is going to come bursting in. Get ready for some
*wow*s in Jesus' Name!

CHAPTER THREE

Secret Frustrations

A young lady I know volunteers at Lakewood on our prayer team. She and her husband have been trying to have a baby for years. During our services, she'll pray for people who are also trying to have a child. Again and again the people she prays for have come back with their babies in their arms, so happy and fulfilled. She sees their prayers get answered, but her own prayer has not been answered. This young lady looks as though she has it all. She's beautiful and successful and has a great husband, but what you can't see is that secret frustration, that one thing she can't understand.

Life is full of seeming contradictions like this that try to keep us in the darkness. You're helping other people get well, but you don't feel well. Your coworkers keep getting promoted, and though you're working just as hard, producing just as much, nobody notices you. All of us have secret frustrations—things that we know God could change. We know He could open the door, or He could remove the temptation, or He could give us the baby we're dreaming about, but it's not happening. It's easy to get stuck with the "why" questions.

We have to realize that God is a sovereign God. We're not going to understand why everything happens or doesn't happen. There are some things God doesn't remove. There are some situations that He waits a long time to change. You have to trust that He knows what's best for you. If you keep the right attitude, all those frustrating situations that are not changing and afflictions that He's not removing won't work against you, but instead will work for you. Don't let the contradictions of life cause you to get sour and give up on your dreams.

Don't let the contradictions of life cause you to get sour and give up on your dreams.

Making Grace Our Sufficiency

The apostle Paul, who wrote about half the books of the New Testament, talked about these secret frustrations. He was highly educated and came from an influential family. God used Paul in a great way, but, as effective as Paul was, he had a secret frustration. He called it "a thorn in the flesh." Scholars have debated whether it was a physical condition such as an illness, an emotional issue, the persecution he often endured, or the people who were constantly coming against him. Whatever that thorn was, whatever was bothering him, Paul prayed three times for God to remove it. One translation of the Scripture says he "implored" God to take it away. That means that Paul gave it his best argument. "God, I've served You. I've been my best. I've prayed for others, and they've been healed. God, please heal me. I'm tired of this thorn, and I'm tired of people treating me wrongly because of it. God, please take it away." If anybody ever had pull with God, it was Paul. But what's interesting is that God never removed that thorn. Paul wrote in 2 Corinthians 12 that God's answer to him was, "My grace is sufficient for you. My power shows up greatest in weakness."

Is there something you've implored God to change, perhaps a situation in your health, your finances, a relationship? You've asked again and again, but nothing's improved. I'm not saying to give up and settle there in a dark place. What I'm saying is that if God is not removing it or changing it, don't let it steal your joy, don't let it sour your life. God has given you the grace to be there. The right attitude is, *I'm not going to let this secret frustration, this thorn in my flesh, so to speak, frustrate me anymore. God, I know Your grace is sufficient for me. I have the power to be here with a good attitude. I believe that at the right time You will change it; but if it never changes, I'm still going to be my best and honor You.*

You have to make up your mind about what frustrates you. If that issue with your spouse doesn't change, if your health doesn't improve, if you have to put up with that grouchy boss for the rest of your life, if you have to struggle with that temptation till the day you die, you're not going to complain, and you're not going to use it as an excuse to slack off. You're going to tap into this grace. It's sufficient for you. That means you are well able to enjoy your life in spite of these secret frustrations.

Here's a key: don't focus on the frustration. Paul could have gone around thinking, *God, why won't You remove this thorn?* If he had gotten stuck on the whys of life, he would have never fulfilled his destiny. We do the same when we keep asking why God hasn't changed our child or caused our business to grow. Faith is trusting God when life doesn't make sense.

A man named Smith Wigglesworth was one of the

great ministers who lived back in the early nineteen hundreds. He held large meetings where hundreds of people came and were healed. He saw all kinds of miracles. But Wigglesworth suffered most of his life from kidney stones. There were times when he would go home after a service in so much pain that he couldn't walk. He'd lie on his floor hour after hour, trying to get relief. Here he'd just seen great miracles, but he didn't receive his own miracle. Like Paul, he could have been bitter and thought, *This is not right, God. You healed them, and You could heal me. This isn't fair.* Instead he had this attitude: *Your grace is sufficient for every situation. Even when I don't understand, even when it doesn't seem fair, I'm still going to trust You. I'm not going to let this secret frustration keep me from my destiny.*

If you're going to reach your full potential, you can't be a weakling. You have to be a warrior. There will be things you don't understand, things that don't make sense, but God knows what He's doing. His ways are better than our ways. His thoughts are higher than our thoughts. He is the Potter, and we are the clay. If it's supposed to be removed, He'll remove it. If not, dig your heels in and fight

> *If you're going to reach your full potential, you can't be a weakling. You have to be a warrior.*

the good fight of faith. You have the grace you need for every situation.

Why We May Need to Carry Our Bed

When Jesus healed a man who had been crippled for thirty-eight years, He told him to get up off the ground, take up his bed, and walk (see John 5). It's significant that He told him to take his bed with him. He could have said, "Just get up and be on your way." After all, the man didn't need his bed anymore. But Jesus was saying, "The thing that held you back, the thing that kept you for years from being your best, I want you to take that with you as a reminder of what I've done in your life." Even though he could walk and didn't need the bed, it remained a part of his life. It was a contradiction. "I'm blessed, but I still have this bed. I'm happy, but I'm still carrying this bed." I can imagine him helping somebody else who was struggling. They would look at him and say, "How can you help me? You still have that bed. You're still carrying around that thing that held you back." The man said, "This is not what you think. It's not a limitation to slow me down. It's a testimony of what God has done in my life. This bed looks like a liability, but really it's an asset. Every time I see it, it reminds me to give God praise. It reminds me of the dark place He brought me from, and it reminds me that if He did it for me once, He'll do it for me again."

What I'm saying is that even though God frees you from certain things, you may still have your bed. You may still feel tempted in that same area. The weakness, the limitation, may not totally go away. But the reason God didn't remove the bed wasn't that He wanted to slow you down or give you an excuse to fall back, but rather that He wanted it to be a reminder of where you came from. That bed is not there to discourage you but to inspire you.

I've been ministering now for seventeen years. When I first started, I was insecure and intimidated and felt unqualified. Over these last years I've grown, I've gotten more confident, and I've come to better understand who I am. But the truth is, God didn't make me into a different person. When I get up to speak, you may not see it, but I still have my bed. Those limitations and those weaknesses didn't all go away. I still feel them sometimes, but I see them in a new light. They don't intimidate me now; rather, they remind me of my dependency on God.

The reason He doesn't always remove the bed is that when you think you can do it on your own, and you think you have it all figured out, you'll end up right back where you were. But if you'll see your weakness, your temptation, as a reminder to ask God for His help and to thank Him for what He's done, then you'll continue to move forward in spite of what's come against you. I can say now, "Yes, I have my bed, but I'm pastoring the church. I have my bed, but I'm helping other people. I have my bed, but I'm enjoying life, and I'm healthy and whole and blessed."

Walk in the Place of Peace

In the Old Testament, God told Moses to go tell Pharaoh to let the people of Israel go. Moses was insecure; after forty years in the wilderness taking care of sheep, he didn't feel qualified. He said, "God, how will they know that You sent me? I don't have any influence. Why would they believe me?" God told him to throw his staff to the ground, and when he did, it became a snake. When Moses picked the snake up, it turned back into a staff. Then God told him to put his hand into his coat. When he pulled his hand out, it was full of leprosy. After he put it in again and pulled it out again, his hand was perfectly normal. God showed Moses these signs so that he would go into the courts of Pharaoh with confidence, knowing that God was with him.

But Moses had another concern. He said, "God, You've shown me these great signs, but I can't stand before Pharaoh because I stutter and stammer. I have a problem with my speech." You would have thought, since God just did all those miracles, He would simply touch Moses' tongue and take away the stuttering. But God didn't do it. He didn't remove that problem. God was saying to Moses what He said to Paul: "My strength is made perfect in your weakness. If I needed to remove it for you to fulfill your destiny, I would have removed it."

> *"My strength is made perfect in your weakness."*

Are you waiting for God to remove something before you can be happy, before you can pursue a dream, finish school, or be good to somebody? You have what you need. If God is not removing it, it's not an accident. If He's not changing what you want changed, there is a reason. You may not be able to see it, it may not make sense to you, but you have to trust Him. God has your best interests at heart. You're not supposed to live frustrated because a problem isn't turning around. Don't live stressed out because a family member is not doing right or be upset because a dream is taking too long. Come back to that place of peace.

Tried in the Fire of Affliction

The Scripture talks about how we have treasure "in earthen vessels." Yet all of us have imperfections within our clay pot—seeming contradictions. There's something that's not being removed or changed that could easily irritate us and cause us to live frustrated. What is it for you? Perhaps you say, "If I didn't have this back pain or this weight problem, I would be happy." It might be a coworker who gets on your nerves, or a mother-in-law who won't leave and stop interfering. You may have a legal problem or a financial situation that hasn't gone away. For many people, it's the hurts from going through a bad childhood, then a divorce.

Whatever your thorn is, God is saying to you what He said to Paul: "My grace is sufficient. Quit fighting it. Quit letting it steal your joy." When God is ready to remove it, He will; but until then, you have to tap into that grace and say, "God, my life is in Your hands. You know what I want, and You know what's bothering me. You know my goals and my dreams. If You're not removing it, I may not like it, and I may not understand it, but God, I trust in You."

Here's a key: if God is not removing it, there's a reason. Nothing happens by accident. Paul thought the thorn in his flesh was to keep him from getting proud, to keep him from getting puffed up because of the great revelations he had been given. Only God knows the reason He allows thorns to remain in our lives. That secret frustration may just be for a time of testing. It may be for a time when you have to prove to God that you're going to be content and do your best when things are not going your way. You're going to keep giving even when you're not receiving. You're going to keep trying when every door is closing. You're going to keep doing the right thing even when you're not seeing right results.

God may be using that thorn to develop your character and grow you up. Some things you can only learn in the trial of affliction. You can't learn them by reading a book or listening to a message. You have to experience them. The Scripture says, "I have tried you in the fire of affliction." That place of testing is where your spiritual muscles are developed. You can't get stronger without working out and exercising those muscles during times of intense pressure. That can be uncomfortable, it's not easy, and we don't like it. But if we stay with it, it will work for us, not against us. We will be growing, getting stronger, being prepared for new levels.

You can't be promoted without preparation. God won't give you a hundred-pound blessing when He knows you can lift only fifty pounds. If He gave

Your gifts may take you to a certain level, but if you don't have the character to match them, you won't stay there.

you the hundred pounds, it wouldn't be a blessing; it would be a burden. He has to get you prepared. Your gifts may take you to a certain level, but if you don't have the character to match them, you won't stay there. Character is developed in the tough times, when you're not getting your way but you keep doing the right thing.

As Paul did, we've all asked, "God, please remove this secret frustration." "Remove this person at work who gets on my nerves." "Change my spouse and make him more loving." "Give me the baby we've been praying for." Until God changes it, if you'll keep doing the right thing, not letting it sour you, not getting frustrated, not giving up, then here's the beauty of it: even if the situation never changes, you will change. You're getting stronger, you're coming up higher, you're being prepared for the fullness of your destiny.

Let Your Character Be Developed

I've learned that our character is more important than our talent. We can have all the talent in the world, but if we don't have strong character, we won't go very far. We can all trust God in the good times—that's easy. But can you trust Him with the secret frustrations, the things that haven't changed? You've prayed and believed, but God hasn't removed it. The question is not only if you can trust God but, more important, if God can trust you. Will you pass that test and stay in faith even when you don't understand it?

My father started Lakewood in 1959 with ninety people. A few years later, he left the church, having put somebody else in charge, so he could travel around the world. He would hold big crusades in other countries with crowds of fifty thousand people. He saw God do amazing things. He was living his dream. But at one point he knew he was supposed to come back and pastor Lakewood again. My mother said, "John, when Houston hears you're back, they're going to be so thrilled! They're going to come out by the thousands." Well, Houston heard, but Houston didn't care. They stayed away by the thousands! Instead of preaching to the huge crowds that he'd become used to, he was speaking to ninety people, three times a week, year after year. Down deep my father had this secret frustration. "God, I'm made for more than this. I'm being my best, I'm honoring You, but I'm not seeing growth. Nothing is changing."

What my father didn't realize was that something was changing—not the size of the congregation, but he himself. He was developing character; he was proving to God that he would be faithful in the tough times. On the outside my father was happy, and there was never a question about whether he gave his all to those ninety people. But down deep inside, he had to deal with this secret frustration. "God, why isn't the church growing?" Then, in 1972, it was as though somebody opened up a faucet and people started pouring in from all parts of the city. Lakewood grew and grew to a church of thousands. God had used the dark place to bring my father into abundant blessing.

Like my father, maybe you're doing the right thing, but your secret frustration is not changing—you're not seeing any growth, you're not being promoted. Nothing may be happening on the outside, but if you keep the right attitude, something is happening on the inside. God is changing you. Keep doing the right thing, keep being good to people, keep giving it your best and having an excellent spirit. God is growing you up. You're being prepared for promotion. Too many people

> *Nothing may be happening on the outside, but if you keep the right attitude, something is happening on the inside.*

let these secret frustrations cause them to get sour, lose their passion, and slack off. Recognize that what you're facing is a test. If you'll keep doing the right thing, God will get you to where you're supposed to be.

A Tale of Two Sisters

In Genesis 29–30 is the story of two sisters named Rachel and Leah. When a young man named Jacob saw Rachel, he fell head over heels for her. It was love at first sight. Rachel was extremely attractive. The Scripture says, "She was beautiful in every way, with a lovely face and shapely figure." When God says you're fine, you really have it going on. Jacob didn't have to think twice—he was in love. He asked her father, Laban, if he could marry her. Laban said, "Yes, but you have to first work for me for seven years."

Jacob worked those seven years and was very excited, but Laban tricked Jacob. At weddings back then, the brides wore veils so thick that you couldn't tell who was under them. Jacob assumed he was getting Rachel, but instead it was Leah. The Scripture says, "Leah's eyes were weak and dull looking." I'm not sure what "weak" means in reference to eyes, but I know what "dull looking" is. No offense to Leah, but Rachel got the looks in the family.

At the wedding they probably had a little too much to drink. In any case, Jacob woke up the next morning, looked over in bed, and there were weak eyes staring back at him. He nearly passed out. He ran back to Laban and said, "What do you mean giving me Leah? That's not the deal we made!" Laban answered, "I know, but our tradition says the older sister has to be married off first. Work for me another seven years, and I'll give you Rachel as well." Jacob did that and was finally able to marry Rachel.

I'm sure that when people saw Rachel around town, so friendly, so beautiful, they thought, *That's one blessed lady. She's stunning, has a husband who adores her, and comes from a good family.* But what they couldn't see was that Rachel had a secret frustration. Her dream was to have a baby, but she was barren and stuck in a really dark place. She couldn't conceive a baby, and year after year went by with no children. I can hear her saying every night, "God, please give me a child. God, please remove this barrenness. I want to have a baby."

On the other hand, her sister, Leah, gave Jacob one son after another, six strong, handsome boys as well as one beautiful daughter. Life seemed good for Leah. Her dream had come to pass, and God had blessed her with a healthy family. However, Leah too had a secret frustration, an equally dark place. The Scripture says, "Jacob loved Rachel more than Leah." Leah was so proud of her sons and daughter, they brought so much joy to her life, but I can hear her saying every night, "God, this is so painful. Why doesn't Jacob love me more? Why don't You change his heart?"

The point is, everybody is dealing with a secret frustration. Whether you're Rachel, blessed in one area, or Leah, blessed in another, there will be things that frustrate you, things you don't understand, things God is not removing. You have to make up your mind that you're not going to let it sour your life; you're not going to live frustrated. Do

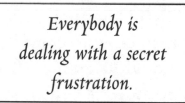

Everybody is dealing with a secret frustration.

what you can, but trust God to do what you can't. The right attitude is, *God, if it never changes, if I never have children, I'm still going to be happy. If my marriage never improves, I'm not going to live sour. If somebody looks better than I, has more than I, is more talented than I, I'm not going to be jealous or bitter. I'm at peace with who I am.*

When you live in peace, you won't be trying to figure out why someone else got the looks or someone else has all the children, or be trying to get your husband to love you more. You give it to God. At the right time God will remove what's supposed to be removed. He'll change what's supposed to be changed. That's what happened with Rachel. Years later God removed the barrenness, and she had a remarkable son named Joseph. The darkness gave way to the light, and that secret frustration gave way to a huge blessing.

Whether It Changes or Not

For most of my father's life, he struggled with high blood pressure. He was constantly trying new medicines to control it. Many times the side effects would make him miserable. He was helping people every week, changing lives all over the world, yet he struggled with this sickness. Nobody I have known had more faith than my father, nobody knew the Scripture as he did, but for some reason God never took it away. Yet I never heard my father complain. His attitude was, *God, I'm going to be my best whether or not You heal me of this high blood pressure*. He had a made-up mind. Toward the end of his life, the medicine would make him dizzy, and sometimes he wouldn't sleep all night, but he would come in on Sundays and preach his heart out. He could have thought, *God,*

I've served You for fifty years—the least You could do is answer this prayer. But he didn't let that secret frustration stop him. He trusted God even when things didn't seem to make sense.

At seventy-seven years old, after my father had to go on dialysis, he was still ministering every weekend. One night he couldn't sleep, and he called my brother-in-law Gary and asked him to come visit. Around one in the morning they were talking, and Gary asked my father what he thought about the difficulty he was going through. My father said, "Gary, I don't understand it all, but I know this: His mercy endures forever." Those were the last words my father ever spoke. A few seconds later he had a heart attack and went to be with the Lord. I love the fact that even though God didn't remove the high blood pressure, my father didn't get bitter, and he died in faith. Whatever secret frustration you're dealing with, you have to make the decision that my father made: if it never changes, you're still going to stay in faith.

> *"I don't understand it all, but I know this: His mercy endures forever."*

This is what three Hebrew teenagers did in the Scripture. They wouldn't bow down to the king of Babylon's golden idol. He was so furious that he was about to have them thrown into a fiery furnace. They said, "King, we're not worried. We know that our God will deliver us. But even if He doesn't, we're still not going to bow down." This is the key: you stay in faith, believe in your dreams, believe the situation will turn around, but then take it one step further and declare, "Even if it doesn't happen my way, even if I don't get delivered, I'm still going to be happy. God, if You turn it around, I'm going to give You praise. And if You don't turn it around, I'm still going to give You praise." You live like that and all the forces of darkness cannot keep you from your destiny.

Friend, don't let secret frustrations steal your joy and keep you in a dark place. Have a new perspective. You have the grace for anything you're facing. If God is not removing it, there's a reason. Don't try to figure it out; trust Him. If you'll do this, you will not only enjoy your life more, but God will remove everything that's supposed to be removed, and you will rise higher, overcome obstacles, and become everything you were created to be.

CHAPTER FOUR

Unconditional Trust

It's easy to trust God when things are going our way, we're getting good breaks, our business is blessed, and our children are healthy. We don't need much faith when life is good. But what about when things aren't going our way, our prayers aren't being answered, the problem isn't turning around, and we're not seeing favor? Too often we get discouraged and think, *God, why aren't You doing something? You can see I'm being mistreated. My health isn't good. I worked hard, but I didn't get the promotion.* We think that when it changes, we'll be happy. "When I meet the right person…" "When my health improves…" "When we have our baby, we'll have a good attitude." That's conditional trust. We're saying, "God, if You meet my demands, if You answer my prayers in the way I want and according to my timetable, I'll be my best."

> *The problem with conditional trust is that there will always be things we don't understand, something that's not happening fast enough, something that doesn't work out the way we want.*

The problem with conditional trust is that there will always be things we don't understand, something that's not happening fast enough, something that doesn't work out the way we want. The question is, are you mature enough to accept God's answers even when they're not what you were hoping for? God is a sovereign God. We're not going to understand everything that happens. Faith is trusting God when life doesn't make sense. There will always be unanswered questions. "Why didn't my loved one make it?" "Why am I not getting better?" "Why did this person leave?" Some things are not going to make sense. But God wouldn't have allowed it if He weren't going to bring good out of it. You may not see it at the time, but God knows what He's doing. He has your best interest at heart. It's not random. It's a part of His plan. Dare to trust Him.

From Darkest Hour to Brightest Hour

This is what happened in our family. When my father's health started to go downhill, we prayed just as hard for him as we had for my mother when she had cancer. We quoted the same Scriptures. We asked God to restore his health, to let him live, as He had my mother, but my father went to be with the Lord. It didn't happen the way I wanted. If I'd had conditional trust, I would have gotten upset and bitter and said, "God, why didn't You answer my prayers?" The truth is, God did answer my prayers. Just not the way I wanted.

I didn't want to lose my father, of course. Besides being my dad, he was one of my best friends. I'd worked with him at Lakewood for seventeen years. We had traveled the world together. I didn't know what I would do when he was gone. But I found out that God had another plan. He had something else for me to do. I couldn't see it at the time. I wanted God to do it my way, but God had a better way. I thought I would spend my life behind the scenes, doing the television production, running the cameras. I didn't think I could get up in front of people. I didn't know this ability was in me.

God can see things in you that you can't see in yourself. His plan for your life is bigger than your plan. But it may not happen the way you think. God doesn't take us in a straight line. There will be twists, turns, disappointments, losses, and bad breaks. They're all a part of His plan. But if you have conditional trust, you'll get discouraged and

God doesn't take us in a straight line. There will be twists, turns, disappointments, losses, and bad breaks. They're all a part of His plan.

think, *Why is this happening? I'm going the wrong way.* But God is still directing your steps. Trust Him when you don't understand. Trust Him even when it feels as though you're going in the wrong direction.

What I thought would be my darkest hour, the loss of my father—and I say this respectfully—in one sense turned out to be my brightest hour. It launched me into what I'm doing today, onto a new level of my destiny. But sometimes we so want things our way that we're not going to be happy unless they happen our way. "I can't be happy unless I get the house I want." "Unless I meet the right person." "Unless we have the baby." That's out of balance. Anything you have to have in order to be happy the enemy can use against you. It's good to be honest with God and tell Him your dreams. Tell Him what you're believing for. "God, this is what I want. I'm asking You to heal my loved one. Turn this problem around. God, open these new doors." It's fine to ask, but then be mature enough to say, "But God, if it never happens, if I don't get the promotion, if my loved one doesn't make it, if my health doesn't improve, I'm still going to trust You."

We can get so consumed with what we want that it can become like an idol to us. It's all we think about, all we pray about, always at the forefront of our minds. Turn it over to God. Pray, believe, and then leave it in God's hands. Don't get so focused on what you want that you miss the beauty of this day. Everything may not be perfect. There may be things that need to change. But God has given you the grace to be happy today. It's very freeing when you can say, "God, it's in Your hands. I trust You unconditionally whether it works out my way or not. I trust You unconditionally even when I don't understand it."

"But Even If He Doesn't…"

At the end of the last chapter, I told the story of the three Hebrew teenagers who refused to bow down to the king's golden idol and declared to the king of Babylon, "King, we're not going to bow down. We know that our God will deliver us. But even if He doesn't, we're still not going to bow down." That's unconditional trust. It's saying, "I believe God's going to turn this situation around, but even if He doesn't, I'm still going to be happy. I believe I'm going to get the promotion. I believe my health is improving. I believe the right person is coming. But if it doesn't happen, I'm not going to get bitter or sour. I know that God is still on the throne. If He's not changing it, He has a reason. My life is in His hands."

Dare to trust Him not just when things are going your way, but even when you don't understand it. The psalmist said, "God will work out His plan for your life." You don't have to work it all out. You don't have to make it happen in your own strength, try to manipulate people, or fight all your battles alone. Why don't you relax and take the pressure off yourself and let God work out His plan for your life? He can do it better than you can. He knows the best path. That's what the Hebrew teenagers were saying. "We know God will deliver us from this fire. But even if He doesn't, we're not going to get upset and start panicking. We know we're not doing life on our own. The Most High God, the Creator of the universe, is working out His plan for our lives."

> *You don't have to make it happen in your own strength, try to manipulate people, or fight all your battles alone.*

All the forces of darkness cannot stop what God has ordained. Sickness can't stop Him. Trouble at work can't stop Him. Disappointments and set-backs can't stop Him.

You may have a lot coming against you. You feel as though you're about to be thrown into a fire. The good news is, you're not going to go in there alone. You can't be put in that fire unless God allows it. The enemy is not in control of your life; God is in control. He is working out His plan. Sometimes His plan includes fiery furnaces. Sometimes it includes giants, Red Seas, Pharaohs, and other people who don't like you. Sometimes obstacles will seem insurmountable. You don't see a way, but since you know the Lord is directing your steps, you don't try to figure it all out. It may look like the end, but, like those teenagers, you have unconditional trust. "I know God will deliver me, but even if He doesn't, I'm still going to have a song of praise. I'm still going to have an attitude of faith. I'm still going to live my life happy."

The king had these teenagers thrown into the fiery furnace. The fire was so hot that when the guards opened the door, they were instantly killed. In a few minutes, the king came to check on them. He looked into the furnace and couldn't believe his eyes. He said, "Didn't we throw in three bound men? I see four men loosed, and one looks like the Son of God." What was that? God working out His plan for their lives!

Unconditional Trust

The three Hebrew teenagers were miraculously saved, but I wonder what the outcome would have been if they had had conditional trust. "God, if You deliver us from this fire, we'll stay in faith. God, if You do it our way, we'll keep a good attitude." Maybe the furnace would have been the end. Maybe we wouldn't be talking about them today.

If you want to get God's attention, if you want Him to take you where you've never dreamed and turn impossible situations around, be like those teenagers and have a statement of faith: "I know God will deliver me from this fire." But then follow it up with, "But even if He doesn't, I'm still going to honor Him. I'm still going to be my best." When you live like that, you take away all the enemy's power. If it doesn't work out, he's expecting you to get upset, to be worried, to fall apart, to live

Don't be intimidated. The forces for you are greater than the forces against you.

in self-pity. When you have unconditional trust, you can't be defeated. You may have challenges that look bigger and stronger than you can overcome. On your own, you don't have a chance. Don't be intimidated. The forces for you are greater than the forces against you.

The Scripture says in the book of Job, "You will not be harvested before your time." You may get thrown into a fire, but if it's not your time to go, you're not going to go. God has the final say. Right now He is working out His plan for your life. There may be some fiery furnaces. Are you going to trust Him only if He delivers you from the fire? Only if He takes away all the thorns? Only if He does it your way? Or are you going to have unconditional trust? Will you trust Him like those teenagers even if He takes you through the fire?

When I look back over my life, I see that many things haven't turned out the way I'd thought they would. I had a plan. I had it all figured out. I told God what to do, when to do it, what I needed, whom to use, and how to get me there. I gave Him good information, my very best. The funny thing is, God didn't take my advice. He had His own plan. I found that God's plan is always better than my plan. His ways have always been more rewarding, more fulfilling, and bigger than my ways. If God had done everything I asked, answered my prayers the way I wanted and according to my timetable, it would have limited my destiny. I wouldn't be where I am. I couldn't see it at the time. It didn't make sense. But one day I came to understand the words of the prophet Isaiah: "God's ways are higher than our ways, and His plans are better than our plans."

Quit being discouraged over something that didn't work out the way you wanted. Don't live frustrated because somebody left whom you wanted to stay, or a door closed that you wanted open. God knows what He's doing. You may not see it now, but one day when you see what God was up to, you'll be glad He closed the doors. You'll thank Him for not answering your prayers. The longer I live, the more I pray, "God, let not my will but Your will be done." I don't fight the closed doors anymore. I don't get frustrated when things aren't changing as fast as I would like. I know that God is in control. As long as you're honoring Him and being your best, at the right time God will get you to where you're supposed to be. It may not be where you thought, but God is going to take you further than you ever imagined.

It's All Working for You

I believe in praying for our dreams and praying bold prayers, believing for big things. But I've learned to let God do it His way. Hold tightly to what God put in your heart, but hold loosely to how it's going to happen. Don't get set in your ways. Don't be discouraged because it hasn't happened the way you thought. God is working out His plan for your life.

A few years after Victoria and I were married, we sold our town house and were going to buy our first home. We were so excited. We looked for months and months and finally found a house that we really loved. It was on a beautiful lot with big trees, so picturesque. It was our dream house. We made an offer that was not much less than the sellers were asking. We didn't hear back for a couple of weeks, but the house was empty, so we would go out at night and pray over it, thanking God that it was ours and dreaming about living there. "There's where we'll put our dining room table." "There's where we'll put a swing set one day." We were sure it was going to happen, but the sellers called back and said they weren't going to accept our offer. Well, we knew that had to be the devil trying to take our house because it was supposed to be ours. (Have you noticed the devil gets blamed for a lot of things he has nothing to do with?) We went back to that house and started marching around it, praying, binding, loosing, doing everything we could. A few days later, the owners sold it to somebody else.

Have you ever felt as though God had let you down? He could have changed it so easily. We were right there, but the door closed. We said, "God, where were You? This was our dream house." But if you're only going to be happy if God does it your way, that's not trusting Him; that's giving God orders. You'll be frustrated. Why don't you put your life in His hands? He knows what's best for you. He can see things that we can't see.

A few months later, we found another house close to the city. We purchased that place. A few years after that, we sold half of that property for more than we paid for the whole property. We ended up building a new house there. God blessed us in ways greater than we'd ever imagined. Now sometimes I'll drive back by that other house I wanted so badly and say, "Lord, thank You for closing that door. Thank You that it didn't work out." With some of the things that are not working out in your life now, one day you'll be doing as I did. "Lord, thank You that it didn't work out my way."

You could save yourself a lot of frustration if you'd learn to have unconditional trust. The closed doors, the disappointments, the delays—it's all working for you. And yes, it's good to be determined. Be persistent. But let God do it His way. If He's not changing it, not removing it, not opening it, don't fight it. Learn to embrace where you are. He's given you the grace not just to be there but to be there with a good attitude. If you're going to pass the test, keep a smile on your face. Keep a song in your heart. Keep passion in your spirit. Don't drag through the day disappointed. This is the day the Lord has made. He's still on the throne. He's working out His plan for your life. He's going to get you to where you're supposed to be.

Living worried, frustrated, and disappointed takes our passion, steals our joy, and can keep us from seeing God's favor. Sometimes the closed doors and the disappointments are simply a test. God wants to see if we'll trust Him when we don't understand, when life doesn't make sense.

> *Living worried, frustrated, and disappointed takes our passion, steals our joy, and can keep us from seeing God's favor.*

Pass the Trust Test

This is what happened with Abraham. He was seventy-five years old when God promised him "to become a great nation" (see Gen. 12), and he waited twenty-five years before the birth of his son Isaac. He and his wife, Sarah, had prayed, believed, stood in faith, and finally seen the promise come to pass. They were so excited. You can imagine how Abraham must have felt many years later when God told him to take Isaac to the top of a mountain and sacrifice him. That didn't make sense. Isaac was what Abraham loved the most. Isaac was the fulfillment of the promise God had given him. Now God was asking him to put his dream on the altar. Abraham didn't understand it. It didn't seem fair. But he was obedient. He passed the trust test. And just as he was about to follow through, God stopped him and said, "Abraham, don't do it. Now I can see you trust Me more than anything."

As with Abraham, there will be times when God asks us to put our dream on the altar. We have to show Him that we don't have to have the house

> *Abraham didn't understand it. It didn't seem fair. But he was obedient.*

to be happy. If we don't have the baby, we're not going to live bitter and sour. You're believing for your health to improve, but when you can say, "If it doesn't get better, God, I'm still going to honor You. I'm still going to be my best," you are doing what Abraham did. You are putting your dream on the altar. And when God sees that you don't have to have it, many times God will give you back what you were willing to give up.

During World War II, a writer named S. I. Kishor published a short story in *Collier's* magazine that begins with a young soldier in a library in Florida. While he was reading a used book, he noticed handwritten notes in the margin. They were very thoughtful and heartwarming. He turned to the front of the book, and it just happened to show the previous owner's name, a lady named Hollis Maynell. He got hold of a New York City telephone book and found her address. He wrote her a letter, introducing himself and telling her how he was shipping out to Europe the next day. He invited her to respond, so they could talk about the book. Much to his surprise, he received a letter in return, and for the next thirteen months, they wrote back and forth again and again, getting closer and closer. They were actually falling in love even though they had never seen each other. He had requested a picture, but she'd refused, saying that their looks shouldn't matter if they really cared for each other.

A year and a half later, he was coming back home through New York City. This was their big opportunity. They were going to meet for the first time and go out to dinner. She said, "I'll be waiting for you when you get off the ship. You'll know it's me by the red rose I'll be wearing." Sailing back across the ocean, he was excited and nervous at the same time. He stepped off the ship, and the big moment finally arrived. He saw a beautiful young lady walking toward him who took his breath away. She was stunning—tall, gorgeous features, in great shape. She looked like a movie star. He couldn't believe what he was seeing. When he started toward her, a smile curved her lips, and she said, "Going my way, soldier?" But he was suddenly taken aback when he realized she wasn't wearing a red rose. As she passed by, he finally came back down to earth.

About that time, a lady in her forties walked up to him. She wasn't all that attractive, and she had graying hair, but she was wearing the red rose. Disappointed, but not showing it, he walked up to her with a smile. He saluted and said, "I'm Lieutenant John Blandford, and you—you are Miss Meynell. I'm so glad you could meet me. May—may I take you to dinner?" The lady said, "I don't know what this is all about, son. That young lady in the green suit, who just went by, she asked me to wear this rose on my coat. And she said that if you asked me to go out with you, I should tell you that she's waiting for you in that big restaurant across the street." It had been simply a test.

Will you do the right thing when it's hard? Will you trust God when the situation isn't what you'd thought? Will you trust Him when you don't understand it? God said to Abraham, "Because you did not withhold your only son, I will surely bless you and make your descendants as numerous as the sand on the seashore." When you do as Abraham did, as this young soldier did, and pass the trust test, God will not only give you the desires of your heart, He'll do more than you ask or think.

Are you living frustrated because your prayers aren't being answered the way you want? Your plans aren't working out? Take the pressure off. God is in control. You're not always going to understand it. If you did, it wouldn't take any faith. I'm asking you to trust Him unconditionally. If you'll do this, I believe God is going to work out His plan for your life. He's going to open the right doors, bring the right people to you, turn negative situations around, and take you to the fullness of your destiny.

CHAPTER FIVE

Don't Waste Your Pain

We all go through difficulties, setbacks, and loss. Pain is a part of life, and it often feels like a dark place. It's easy to get discouraged and think, *God, why did this happen to me?* But one of the most important things I've learned is not to put a question mark where God has put a period. All of us live through things we don't understand. One reason is that we can't see the big picture for our lives. If you have a jigsaw puzzle, on the front of the box is the picture that shows you what it's going to look like. Maybe it's a picture of a sunset overlooking the ocean. As a whole it's fantastic, so beautiful. But if you take one piece of that puzzle and isolate it, you'll think, *This piece is a mistake. It's not going to fit anywhere. It's shaped oddly, and there's nothing beautiful about it.* But the fact is, it has a perfect place. It's already been fitted, planned, designed. When all the pieces come together, it's going to fit right in. You just can't see it now because the other pieces are not in place.

In a similar way, sometimes we look at the pieces in our lives that don't make sense. "I lost a loved one." "I went through a divorce." "I'm fighting cancer." "Joel, my business went under. This piece couldn't be a part of God's plan." You have to trust that even in the painful times—the times when you're hurting, you're lonely, you're undergoing medical treatment, and when on the surface the pieces of your life don't make sense—even then, God doesn't make any mistakes. He's already designed your life and laid out every piece, down to the smallest detail. He never said we would understand everything along the way. God didn't promise that there wouldn't be any pain, suffering, or disappointment. But He did promise that it would all work out for our good. That piece that's painful, that doesn't look as though it makes sense—when everything comes together, it's going to fit perfectly in place.

The key is what you do in your times of pain. Pain will change us. Difficulties, heartache, suffering—they don't leave us the same. When I went through the loss of my father, I didn't come out of that experience the same person. I was changed. If you go through a divorce or a legal battle, or have a friend who betrays you, eventually the experience will pass and you will get through it, but you will be different. How the pain changes you is up to you. You can come out bitter, or you can come out better. You can come out with a chip on your shoulder, saying, "Why did this happen?" Or you can come out stronger with a greater trust in God. You can come out defeated, having given up on your dreams, or you can come out blessed with a new fire, looking for the new opportunities in front of you.

We all experience pain. My challenge is, don't just go through it; grow through it. That difficulty is an opportunity to get stronger, to develop character, to gain a greater trust in God. Anybody can fall apart; anybody can get bitter—that's easy. But what that's doing is wasting your pain. That pain is not there to stop you; it's there to develop you, to prepare you, to increase you.

> *That pain is not there to stop you; it's there to develop you, to prepare you, to increase you.*

No Pain, No Gain

The Scripture talks about how God is not only in control of our lives, He's in control of the enemy.

Satan had to ask for permission from God before he could test Job. The enemy may turn on the furnace, but the good news is that God has His hand on the thermostat. God controls how much heat, how much pain, how much adversity we will face. He knows what we can handle. If it is going to harm us rather than help us, He dials it back. In those tough times, when it's uncomfortable, when you're dealing with an illness or going through a loss, you could easily let it overwhelm you. It's helpful to remind yourself, "I may be in the furnace, but I know who's controlling the temperature. The God who breathed His life into me, the God who is for me and not against me, the God who crowned me with favor, the God who takes pleasure in prospering me, He's in complete control. He's not going to let it get too hot. He's not going to let it defeat me. I may not like it, but I'm not a whiner. I'm a warrior. I know I can handle it." You have that attitude, and you're going to come out refined, purified, prepared, and stronger.

You've heard the saying "No pain, no gain." If everything were always easy, we wouldn't be prepared for our destiny. Some of the situations and pressures that I face today would have overwhelmed me if I'd faced them ten years ago. I couldn't have handled it back then. God knows exactly what you need and when you need it. Every struggle is making you stronger. Every difficulty is growing you up. You may not like it, but every painful time is developing something in you that can be developed only in the tough times. Don't complain about the pain, because without the pain you wouldn't reach the fullness of your destiny.

In 1982, researchers aboard the space shuttle *Columbia* did an experiment with honeybees. They took them up into space to study the effects of weightlessness on them. According to a NASA memo, the bees "were unable to fly normally and tumbled into weightlessness." Then it was reported that "the bees have all gotten stationary." One can imagine that they just floated through the air with great ease, having a great time while not having to use their wings. Perhaps they thought, *This is the life. This is the way we were created to live—no struggle, no hardship, no pain.* But they all died. They may have loved having it easy, having no adversity, but they weren't created for that. You might say that they enjoyed the ride, but they died.

Like those bees, we weren't made to float through life on flowery beds of ease. We're going to the sweet by-and-by, but we're living in the nasty now-and-now. We'd love to not have any pain, suffering, bad breaks, betrayals, or loss, but that's not reality. Difficulties will come, and pain is a part of life, so keep the right perspective. In the tough dark times, God is getting you prepared.

> *The reason the fire is so hot is that there's something big in your future.*

If it were too much, God would dial back the intensity. He has His hand on the thermostat. Quit telling yourself that you can't take it. You're not weak. You are well able. You are full of can-do power. You are armed with strength for this battle. The reason the fire is so hot is that there's something big in your future. God is growing you up. He's getting you ready to receive blessings, favor, and increase as you've never seen.

There Is a Lesson in the Pain

There is purpose in your pain. God allows the pain, but He doesn't say, "Let Me give them some pain to make their life miserable. Let Me hit her with this sickness, and let Me cause him some heartache." He uses it for a purpose. We're not always going to understand it. "Why did I get sick? Why did my loved one not make it? Why did my marriage not work?" I can't answer the whys, but I can tell you that if God allowed it, He knows how to bring good out of it. This is what faith is all about. "God, I don't like this pain and darkness, but I trust You. I believe You're in control. I'm not just going to go through it, I'm going to grow through it. I'm going to keep a good attitude. I'm going to count it all joy, knowing that this pain is going to lead to my gain."

Sometimes we bring the pain on ourselves. We make poor choices, get into a relationship that we knew would not be good, or get in over our head in our spending, and then there's the pain—we're dealing with the consequences. God is full of mercy, and He'll always give us the grace to get through it. But in order not to waste the pain, you have to learn the lesson. Be big enough to say, "Here's where I missed it. I ignored the warnings, and I got involved with the wrong people. I got out of God's timing, but I'm not going to do that again." There's a lesson in that pain. Don't be a hardhead and keep going through the same pain again and again.

A man I know struggled with diabetes for years and ended up in the hospital for a month. I saw him in the lobby afterward and he looked better than ever. He said, "Joel, that time in the hospital was a wake-up call. I've lost forty pounds and changed my diet. I exercise every day and feel like a new man." What is he doing? He's not wasting the pain. He learned the lesson.

We talk about how important it is to let go of the past, to let go of the divorce, the failure, the bad break, and that's true. But before you let go of the negative event, you need to remember the lesson that you learned from the experience. You're doing yourself a disservice if you go through a painful time and

> *Before you let go of the negative event, you need to remember the lesson that you learned from the experience.*

don't come out with what you were supposed to gain. I talked to a man who was about to get married for the fourth time. I'm not judging him, and I don't know his story, but he made one statement that was very telling. He said, "Joel, pray for me. All my wives have run around on me." I didn't say it, but I thought, *The one common denominator in this is you.* Maybe the lesson he needs to learn is to be careful about the kind of women to whom he gravitates.

There's a lesson in the pain. Don't keep repeating the same mistakes. Consider a guy who was driving his car, had an accident, and got out upset. He went over to the other driver and said, "Lady, why don't you watch where you're going? You're the fifth person who's run into me today!" He's going to keep experiencing that pain until he gets big enough to look inside and say, "You know what, I have to learn how to drive." Are you bringing pain on yourself? Are you struggling with relationships that don't last, perhaps because you keep saying everything you feel like saying? The pain will stop if you learn the lesson and zip it up.

The Birth of Something New

Sometimes we experience pain that has nothing to do with our choices. It isn't our fault. We are doing the right thing, and the wrong thing happens.

At forty-eight years of age, my mother was raising five children and pastoring the church with my father, and life was good. She was diagnosed with terminal cancer. Not only was that physically uncomfortable, it was emotionally painful, making her think about leaving her children, leaving her husband. My mother didn't get depressed or bitter. She had learned that where God puts a period, she shouldn't put a question mark. She said, "God, my life is in Your hands. You said the number of my days You will fulfill. I know that people don't have the final say; You have the final say." It didn't happen

The very thing that tried to destroy her was what God used to push her to a new level of her destiny.

overnight, but my mother got better and better. Today not only is she healthy and whole but, out of that difficulty, out of that painful time, God birthed something new in her. She started going around praying for other people who were sick. The very thing that tried to destroy her was what God used to push her to a new level of her destiny. She goes up to the medical center every week and has healing services in the chapel. What the enemy means for your harm, God will use to your advantage.

There are times when God will allow us to go through a painful season so He can birth something new on the inside. Paul said in 2 Corinthians, "The God of all comfort, who comforts us in our time of trouble, so we can comfort those in need, with the comfort we have received." If you go through something you don't understand, instead of getting upset and asking, "God, why me?" have a new perspective. God allowed this to happen because He trusts you. He knows He can count on you to take the same comfort, the same healing, the same encouragement that helped you overcome this trouble, and share it with others. Even though my mother's struggle with cancer was very difficult, she said she wouldn't trade it. She wouldn't have it any different. The pain was for a greater purpose.

Maybe you've gone through something you don't understand—sickness, abuse, infertility, raising a difficult child. It's painful. Life didn't turn out the way you'd hoped. It's easy to have a victim mentality and think, *If God is good, why did this happen to me? Why did those people mistreat me growing up? Why did I have this bad break?* It's because God knows He can trust you with it. The forces of darkness wanted to take you out, but God had His hand on the thermostat. God said, "Not so fast. That's My son, that's My daughter. I have an assignment for them." God told Satan, "You can test My servant Job, but you can't take his life. He's not going to quit serving Me. I know Job." And God is saying this about you: "It's difficult, but I know what you're made of. It's painful, it's not fair, but in the end I'm not only going to bring you out stronger, increased, and promoted, but I'm going to use you to help others who are struggling in that same area." There is purpose in your pain. Do you know how many businesses, ministries, and charities were birthed out of someone's pain?

Turn the Pain Around as a Force for Good

In May 1980, Candy Lightner received a phone call telling her that her thirteen-year-old daughter

Cari had been hit by a car while walking to church. Cari lost her life that day. This mother was devastated and didn't think she could go on. But then she found out the man driving the car had been under the influence of alcohol and was a repeat offender. Something rose up in Candy that she had never felt—a mother's rage. In her late daughter's bedroom, she started an organization with no money, no influence, and no experience. She called it Mothers Against Drunk Driving (MADD). Thirty-seven years later, it is one of the country's largest activist organizations and has saved hundreds of thousands of lives, changed laws, and influenced public awareness and policy.

Candy Lightner understands the principle we're discussing. She didn't waste her pain. No, her efforts didn't bring her daughter back, but she knew there was a purpose in that pain. She could have sat around in the dark place of self-pity and given up on her dreams, but she didn't put a question mark where God had put a period. That piece in her puzzle didn't make any sense to her at the time, but she believed that when everything came together, it would fit perfectly into place. That's what happened. Today she's affecting the world. The enemy meant her experience for harm, but God used it for good.

Most of us are not going to experience something that tragic, but if Candy can take one of life's greatest pains and turn it around to become a force for good, then you and I can find the purpose in our pain. Don't get caught up wondering, "Where does this piece of my puzzle go? It's ugly, and it doesn't make sense." Keep moving forward. Go out as she did and find somebody you can help. Healing comes when you get outside yourself and help others. As long as you stay focused on your pain, what you lost, what didn't work out, you're going to get stuck. There's a blessing in that pain. You are uniquely qualified. You have something to give others. You can comfort those who are going through what you've been through.

> *As long as you stay focused on your pain, what you lost, what didn't work out, you're going to get stuck.*

I know a lady who got a bad medical report. The doctors found what they thought was a cancerous tumor. We prayed and believed that the test would come back negative, but it confirmed that the tumor was indeed cancerous. She's been coming to Lakewood for a long time. She knows she's not a victim; she's a victor. She understands this principle, that there's a purpose to the pain, that God wouldn't have allowed it if He weren't going to bring good out of it. She didn't get negative or bitter. Her attitude was, *God, I trust You. I know I'm in the palms of Your hands. This piece of my puzzle doesn't make sense to me, but I know You have it all figured out, and in the end it's all going to work for my good.* She took the chemo for one year. It was difficult, and she didn't like it, but today she is eleven years cancer-free. Now she goes back to the hospital as a volunteer and encourages other people fighting cancer. She tells them, "I know what you're going through. I've been there. I've taken the chemo. God brought me through it, and He can do it for you." She's not wasting her pain. Her test has become her testimony.

We've all been through things that were uncomfortable, things we didn't like, but God made a way where we didn't see a way. If it weren't for His goodness, His mercy, and His strength, we wouldn't be here. God is counting on us to let our light shine through the dark places. What you've been through will help somebody else get through it. Be on the lookout for others you can encourage.

My friend Coach Dale Brown told me about a young lady named Lolo Jones, a star sprinter and two-time World Indoor Champion in the sixty-meter hurdles. She went to the 2008 Olympics heavily favored to win the gold medal in the hundred-meter hurdles. Nobody had even gotten close to her time. She lined up on the track, the starter fired the gun, and she took off running. Everything was going great, and she was out in front, just as expected. Eight hurdles down; two to go, and she wins the gold. But on the ninth hurdle, her timing was off, and against all odds, she hit the hurdle and slightly fell. It was just enough of a stumble to allow the woman next to her to pass her. She didn't win the gold. She had worked her whole life for that twelve-second race, and it ended with a huge disappointment. In an interview she said, in effect, "I'm very disappointed. It's very painful, but I know now I can help other people who have fallen." What is she doing? She's not wasting her pain.

When you've been through something, in one sense you've been given a gift. You're uniquely qualified to help somebody else in that situation. Quit feeling sorry for yourself and go lift somebody else up. Everything that happens to us happens for a reason. Nothing is a coincidence. Some experiences help us grow, mature, and come up higher. Then there are times when God will allow us to go through a difficult time so later on we can be instrumental in helping others overcome.

Can God trust you with pain? Can God trust you to be uncomfortable? Or will you get discouraged and say, "I don't understand why this is happening to

> *What if God has allowed this difficulty so three years down the road you can help somebody else move forward?*

me"? I say this respectfully: it's not all about you. What if God has allowed this difficulty so three years down the road you can help somebody else move forward? Can He trust you? When I lost my father, that was painful. I didn't like it. But you can't imagine how many people tell me, "Joel, when you talk about your father, and how much you loved him, and how you stepped up and kept moving forward, that helped me to move forward when my loved one died." The comfort I received during that loss I now can pass on to others. We all have something to give. We've all been through loss, pain, and struggle. Don't say to yourself, *Oh, this is so bad*. You may not like it, but there's a purpose to the pain.

For the Joy Set before You

I saw a story on the news about a woman who had been perfectly healthy, but started feeling nauseated. She didn't know what was wrong. Over the next few months her back started hurting, and her feet were swelling. She couldn't sleep well at night. She went to the doctor early on, and the doctor thought it was some kind of virus that would pass. Month after month, different symptoms popped up. She was uncomfortable, swollen, gaining weight. She didn't like it. One day she started having a sharp pain in her stomach area. She tried to endure it, hoping it would pass, but it got worse and worse. Finally, when she was in pain so excruciating that she couldn't take it any longer, her husband rushed her to the emergency room. The doctor examined her and said, "I know now exactly what the problem is." Ninety minutes later, she delivered her first baby boy. She had been pregnant and hadn't known it. All those symptoms that she had been feeling—the pain, the discomfort, the nausea, not sleeping well—there had been a purpose to them. A change had been taking place, and she was about to birth something new.

Like her, there are many times when we're pregnant but we don't know it. All we feel is the pain. "This is uncomfortable. Why is this happening to me?" The pain is a sign that you're about to give birth. If you'll stay in faith, the pain will pass, and you'll give birth to new strength, new talents, new ministry, new business, new relationships. You won't come out the same. There's a purpose to that pain. When you're in a difficult season, and you don't understand it, don't focus on the pain. Focus on the fact that a new level is coming. The Scripture says, "Jesus endured the pain of the cross, looking forward to the joy that was set before Him." If you just focus on the present pain, you'll get discouraged and think, *This is not fair. I can't take this anymore.* Have a new perspective and say, "Yes, this is difficult, and it's not what I had planned, but I know this pain is not here to defeat me. It's here to promote me. It's a sign that I'm about to give birth."

This is what my friends Craig and Samantha did. At the time Craig was the head of our children's ministry. He and Samantha had two beautiful children, and she was expecting a third. When little baby Connor was born, they soon realized something wasn't right. As he grew, he wasn't developing or talking as their other children had. Connor was diagnosed with autism. Of course they loved Connor unconditionally, but it wasn't what they had been expecting. They were discouraged, but Craig and Samantha understand the principle. They didn't put a question mark where God had put a period. They knew they had been given Connor because God could trust them. They didn't waste their pain. Craig talked to me about how there was no place for special needs children at our church. Parents couldn't come and attend a service if their children required constant attention. He said, "Why don't we start a special needs class? We can call it the Champions Club."

He recognized in that painful time that he was pregnant and that God was about to deliver something new. We started the Champions Club, and within the first few months, three hundred new families joined the church! Then other churches heard about it, and Craig helped them launch their own special needs ministries. Today there are over thirty Champions Clubs in seven different nations.

When it's painful, don't get discouraged. Get ready, because you're about to give birth. That discomfort you're feeling, it's not just a random pain—that's a birth pain. There's a gift in that pain. There's a ministry in that pain. There's a blessing in that pain. Don't waste it. Look for opportunities. As with Craig, God is counting

Can God trust you with pain?

on you to help others facing the same thing. Can God trust you with pain? Will you get bitter and give up on your dreams, or will you say, "God, I may not understand this, but I trust You."

Remember, God has His hand on the thermostat. He wouldn't allow the intense fire if He didn't have a purpose. Don't just go through it, grow through it. If you'll do this, your pain is going to be turned into your gain. You're going to come out stronger, promoted, and increased. Out of that pain you're going to give birth to a new level of your destiny.

CHAPTER SIX

Blessed by Your Enemies

We all know that God can bless us. He can show us favor, promote us, heal us. But what we don't always realize is that God can use our enemies to bless us. What you think is a disappointment someone has caused—that person who left you, that coworker who's trying to make you look bad, that friend who betrayed you—you may not like it, but you couldn't reach your destiny without it. It's all a part of God's plan to get you to where you're supposed to be.

If it weren't for Goliath, David would be known only as a shepherd boy. Goliath was strategically placed in David's path—not to defeat him, but to promote him. Without Goliath, David would have never taken the throne. Don't complain about your enemies. What may look like a setback is really a setup to get you to your throne. God could have used King Saul, who had the authority, to promote David. All God had to do was move on Saul's heart and tell him, "Promote that young man." But God chose to bless David through his enemies in this case, not through his friends. That's why we don't have to play up to people and try to convince them to like us, thinking, *Maybe they'll give me a good break.* God doesn't have to use your friends or associates. He can use your enemies, your critics, the people who are trying to push you down. He'll use them to push you up.

After David defeated Goliath, you never read anything more about Goliath. He was created for David's purpose. Part of his destiny was to establish who David was. In the same way, God has lined up divine connections, people who will be good to you, encourage you, and push you forward. He's also lined up people who will try to stop you, people who will try to make you look bad and discourage you. There are Goliaths ordained to come across your path. If you don't understand this principle, you'll get discouraged and think, *God, why is this happening to me?* That opposition is not there to stop you; it's there to establish you. When you overcome, not only will you step up

> There are Goliaths ordained to come across your path.

to a new level of your destiny, but everyone around you will see the favor of God on your life.

When Goliath Steps in Front of You

In 2002 we received word that the Houston Rockets were moving out of the Compaq Center and the city leaders were thinking about selling it. We needed and had been looking for a larger auditorium. When I heard this news, something came alive inside me. I knew that building was supposed to be ours. Word got out in the city that we were interested in it. There was a lot of talk about what should happen to this building.

A friend of mine was at a luncheon with some local high-powered business executives. One of the executives, a very influential man, found out that my friend attends Lakewood. This executive began to talk about the Compaq Center and how opposed he was to our buying it and what a terrible thing that would be for the city. He said that it should remain a sports arena, and that by no means should the city allow a church there, and on and on. Some of the other people at the table joined in, laughing about it, making fun, saying we didn't have a chance in the world to get it. Finally the executive looked at my friend and said sarcastically, "It will be a cold day in hell before Lakewood gets that building." My friend called me afterward and told me about the discussion. I thought, *Thanks a lot for the good news!* But the truth is, that discussion was ordained by the Creator. That executive was one of those Goliaths whom God strategically places in our path.

When I heard how much he was against us, something rose up inside me. I had been determined before, but now there was a holy determination. I had a new fire, a new passion, a new resolve. Every time things got tough and I was tempted to get discouraged and to think it wasn't going to work out, I would recall his words, *a cold day in hell*, and instantly get my passion back. Sometimes God will put an enemy in your life to keep you stirred up. He'll allow critics, naysayers, discouragers, and even some haters, so that when you're tired and feel like giving up, just the thought of them will help you shake it off and keep moving forward—not because you feel like it, but because you don't want to give your enemies the joy of seeing you defeated. Sometimes you'll have a smile on your face, just so that person who hurt you doesn't see you discouraged. This is not because of spite or pride, but a holy determination. God uses the negative to keep us stirred up.

Although the business leader who was so against us doesn't realize it, God used him more than he used my friends. He was one of the most instrumental people in our getting the Compaq Center. The funny thing is that he wasn't for us; he was dead set against us. God used our enemy to bless us. If I ever see that man, I need to buy him dinner (McDonald's, I'm thinking). I need to write some of my enemies a check. If they hadn't been against me, I wouldn't have prayed so hard. If they hadn't made fun of us, I might have given up when it seemed overwhelming. If they hadn't tried to push me down, to talk me out of it, and told me I didn't have what it takes, I might have settled where I was. It was their opposition that pushed me forward. Many times your enemies will do more to catapult you to success than your friends.

> *Many times your enemies will do more to catapult you to success than your friends.*

There's a Table Prepared for You

David said to God, "You prepare a table before me in the presence of my enemies." When God brings you through the dark valley of opposition, He's not going to do it in private. He's going to do it in such a way that all your enemies can see He has blessed you. Our building is on the second-busiest freeway in the nation. You can't drive in the city of Houston for very long without seeing what God has done for Lakewood. Every time that man who said we'd never get the Compaq Center drives by, I can imagine something whispers in his ear, "It's a cold day in hell," because we're right there.

You may be up against a similar enemy right now—an enemy to your health, your finances, a relationship. It may look as though it's never going to work out. Have this new perspective: God is preparing the table right now, the angels are taking the food out of the oven, they're setting the place mats, Gabriel is putting the finishing touches on the meal, and any moment you're going to hear the dinner bell. God is going to say, "It's time! Here's the meal I've prepared for you." It's not going to be a little fast-food meal tucked over in the corner where nobody notices. God is going to prepare a table for you as He did for David, as He did for us, where not just all your friends can see it, but even your enemies—the doubters, the critics, the people who said it wouldn't work out—are going to see you blessed, healed, promoted, vindicated, in a position of honor and influence.

In one sense God used Judas more than He used the other disciples. Judas was ordained to betray Jesus—that was his purpose, to try to stop Him. It wasn't just his idea; it was part of the plan of God. At the time it seemed like a bad break, but had he not betrayed Jesus, there wouldn't have been a crucifixion, and without the cross there wouldn't have been a resurrection, and without a resurrection we wouldn't have redemption. We celebrate Mary, the mother of Jesus, giving birth in the manger; we celebrate John baptizing Jesus and the dove coming down from heaven, and we celebrate Peter, James, and John walking with Jesus and being His friends. But at the same time, the man who betrayed Jesus, the one who sold Him out for thirty pieces of silver, was just as critical to His destiny, if not more so than the others.

What am I saying? Don't complain about that person who betrayed you. If they walked away, they didn't set you back; they set you up. If that had not happened, you wouldn't get to where you're supposed to be. If they overlooked you, tried to push you down, and lied about you, it may not have been fair, but nothing happens by accident. If God allowed it, He knows how to use it for your good.

What if Jesus had gotten upset and said, "God, I'm Your Son. How could You allow this man to betray Me? He's one of My main disciples." Jesus knew Judas

Jesus understood that betrayal was a part of His destiny.

was going to betray Him, but He didn't try to stop him. He didn't try to talk him out of it. He said at their last supper together, "The one to whom I give this bread is going to betray Me." He handed it to Judas and said, "Go, do what you're going to do quickly." Jesus understood that betrayal was a part of His destiny. Too often we fight what doesn't go our way; we get upset and become bitter. But the longer I live, the more I realize that nothing happens by accident. If you keep the right attitude, God will even use the opposition to bless you.

The Enemy Will Be Used to Bless You

I talked to a well-known minister one time. For over fifty years he had gone around the world doing so much good. Most people were very appreciative and received him well. But in his hometown, the editors of the local newspaper never liked him. They were constantly finding something bad to write. He could do a hundred things right, but they wouldn't report on that. They would find the one thing they didn't like and make a big deal about it. This went on year after year. He had an interesting perspective. He told me, "If it weren't for that newspaper, I wouldn't have accomplished as much." I asked, "What do you mean?" He answered, "That newspaper not only kept me on my knees, but it gave me the fuel to prove them wrong." This minister went on to build a beautiful university in that city, which tens of thousands of young people have attended. Toward the end of his life, when he was retired, that paper's editors finally had a change of heart. They wrote a big front-page article that celebrated everything he had done. It was as though God had waited on purpose. God knew that enemy, even though my friend didn't like all the criticism, was making him better. It kept him stirred up. He was more determined and more diligent, and couldn't let his guard down.

There are some things we don't like, some things we may even be praying for God to take away from us, but if He removed them, we wouldn't reach our highest potential. That opposition is making you stronger. Those people who try to push you down, the betrayal, the disappointment—none of these can keep you from your destiny. God has the final say. If He hasn't removed it, that means it's working for you. He strategically places the Goliaths, the Judases, the critics, the opposition in our lives. Without Goliath, you won't take your throne; without Judas, you won't reach your destiny; without the naysayers, you won't become all you were created to be.

In the Scripture, four men carried a paralyzed man to see Jesus. When they arrived at the house, it was so crowded inside they had to take him up on the roof and let him down through the ceiling. At one point Jesus said to the man, "Your sins have been forgiven." Some of the religious leaders were offended and began to murmur to themselves. Under their breath, they said, "Who does He think He is? He can't forgive sins. Only God can do that." The Scripture says, "Jesus knew their thoughts." They were trying to be discreet, trying to hide their reaction, but He knew full well what they were thinking. Jesus said to them, "Which is easier to say, 'Your sins are forgiven,' or 'Rise, take up your bed and walk'?" To prove to them that He was the Son of God, He turned to the paralyzed man and told him to rise up. The man stood up, perfectly well. When they saw him stand up, I'm sure the religious leaders nearly passed out. They said to one another, "We've never seen anything like this!"

Here's my point: if the religious leaders had not been murmuring, complaining, criticizing, maybe this man wouldn't have been healed. Jesus could have just forgiven his sins and moved on. But right in the midst of their murmuring, Jesus healed him. When people are talking about you, trying to make you look bad, trying to push you down and keep you in a dark place, don't worry—God sees and hears them. They're putting you in position to be blessed in a greater way. You don't have to straighten them out. Don't get involved in battles that don't matter. Let them talk. Just as with this man, God will use your enemies to bless you. Some of the favor you've seen, some of the good breaks, happened not because of you but because of the people who tried to stop you. They put you in position for promotion.

I always thank God for my friends, but I've learned to thank God for my enemies, too. Without the murmuring, the paralyzed man might not have been healed; without Goliath, David might not have taken the throne; the betrayal of Judas eventually led to the resurrection of Jesus from the grave; without that executive who was against us, we might not have our building. You need to see every enemy, every adversity, every disappointment in a new light: the opposition is not there to defeat you, it's there to increase you, to make you better.

You need to see every enemy, every adversity, every disappointment in a new light: the opposition is not there to defeat you, it's there to increase you, to make you better.

A man told me his business had dwindled down to nothing. It looked as though it wasn't going to make it. To make matters even worse, one of its main competitors had gone on a radio show and talked about it in a very unfavorable light. This competitor had been extremely critical and talked about how this man's business just wasn't up to par. It looked as though that would be the final blow that put this business under. But it was just the opposite. When the competitor talked about it, he drew attention to the business, and things started turning around. New clients started calling, and today it's going stronger than ever. It has even surpassed the competitor's company. What happened? God used the businessman's enemy to bless him. God has all kinds of ways to meet your needs. He can use your critics to promote you. He can cause your obstacles to become stepping-stones. He knows how to take what was meant for your harm and use it to your advantage.

Don't Be Intimidated

In the early nineteen hundreds, cotton farmers in Alabama were facing a major challenge. A tiny insect called the boll weevil had migrated from Mexico to the Cotton Belt, and it was quickly destroying their crops. They tried everything they could to get rid of it. They tried to exterminate it with all kinds of chemicals, and they even came up with a new class of insecticides, but to no long-term avail. Eventually all they could do was sit back and watch their livelihood be eaten away—a very dark place to be in. But one day a farmer had an idea. He said, "Instead of planting our normal cotton crops that we know can't survive, let's plant peanuts." The others looked at him as though he had lost his mind. They said, "Peanuts—we can't make a living off peanuts!" Eventually he convinced them to try it, and they went to work. They discovered that the boll weevils didn't like the taste of peanuts. Their crops took off in a way they had never seen. They made more money off peanuts in a few months than they would normally make all year long. In fact, when the boll weevils were diminished, many of the farmers didn't go back to their normal cotton crops. They stuck with the peanuts. God used the boll weevil to bless them with prosperity. God works in mysterious ways.

You may be dealing with some boll weevils in your life right now. My encouragement is that you stay in faith—peanuts are coming. What you think is a setback is really God setting you up to do something new. Don't sit around complaining about what didn't work out and who did you wrong—that's just

What you think is a setback is really God setting you up to do something new.

a boll weevil. It's something that looks as though it's there to destroy or hurt you, but in fact God sent it to launch you to a new level. The next time you see that person at the office who's always talking about you, trying to make you look bad, just think to yourself, *They're just a boll weevil. They think they're bringing me down, but I know the truth. God is using them to push me up.* God said that He would make your enemies your footstools. That means that when something comes against you—persecution, betrayal, disappointment—instead of letting it be a stumbling block that makes you go down, if you'll stay in faith, God will turn stumbling blocks into stepping-stones that cause you to go up.

When I was ten years old, I played Little League baseball. I was very small for my age. In fact, I was always the smallest player on the team, and people called me Peanut. We were in the middle of an important game, and the stands were full. Everybody was closely watching as I stepped up to bat. When the opposing coach saw how small I was, he stepped out of the dugout and began to holler to his players in the outfield, "Come in closer! Come in closer!" He was waving both arms in the air, making a big scene. He might as well have yelled, "This kid is a loser! He's too small. He's not up to par. He can't hit." Everybody in the stands was watching him. I was standing at home plate, so embarrassed that for a moment I felt like hiding. The outfielders came in right behind the infield. Nobody was in the outfield. All I could think of was that he must have seen my brother, Paul, play!

When I saw the outfield shift the opposing team had put on, something came over me. I thought, *That coach doesn't know who I am. He doesn't know what I can do. He didn't breathe life into me. He doesn't determine my destiny. I am a child of the Most High God. I can do all things through Christ.* I might have been small, but when the pitcher threw the ball, I swung as though I were ten feet tall and gave it everything I had. I connected perfectly and that ball took off, went way over their heads, took two bounces, and hit the fence. Because nobody was in the outfield, I made an inside-the-park home run!

Here's what I want you to see. The next time I got up to bat, that coach stepped out of the dugout with just as much enthusiasm, just as much fanfare, but this time he started hollering to his players, "Back up! Back up! Back up!" I smiled and thought, *Now, I like how that sounds!* In the same way, the enemy will come against you in your thoughts, saying, "You'll never be successful. You'll never break that addiction. You'll never get out of that problem." You can either believe those lies and let him talk you into mediocrity, or you can do as I did as a ten-year-old and say, "No, you don't determine my destiny. You don't set the limits for my life. You didn't give me breath. You don't know what I'm capable of. I may look small, but I'm full of resurrection power." When you rise up in faith like that, you won't be defeated by your enemies—you'll be promoted by your enemies. You do that a few times, and he'll start telling his forces, "Back up! Back up! Back up! He's more powerful than he looks. Don't mess with him. He's highly favored. He's more than a conqueror."

The Scripture says, "Do not be intimidated by your opponents." Don't be intimidated by what somebody says, don't be intimidated by that sickness or by how big the obstacle is. You are not weak, you are not lacking, you are full of can-do power. The greatest force in the universe is on your side.

It May Be Friday, but Sunday Is Coming

After the death of Joseph, the people of Israel living in Egypt were blessed and increased greatly in numbers, to the point that many years later, Pharaoh feared them and put them under slave masters to oppress them with forced labor. But something interesting happened. The Scripture says, "The more Pharaoh afflicted them, the more the Israelites multiplied." Pharaoh thought he was stopping them, but in fact he was increasing them. Sometimes when God wants to promote you, He doesn't send you a good break; He sends you an enemy. He'll cause a Pharaoh, a supervisor perhaps, to turn up the heat. He'll put you in an unfair situation. Don't get discouraged—the more opposition, the more you're going to increase. We may not like it, but we grow under pressure, our character is developed, and we discover talent that we didn't know we had. Pharaoh, by oppressing them with slave labor, was trying to restrict the Israelites, to squeeze them, to put them under pressure.

When you wash your car at home, you know that the water that comes out of your hose is going to shoot only about three or four feet. But when you want to really spray the car off, you need the water to go farther. So you put your thumb over the end of the hose and restrict the flow of the water. You might think that when you restrict it, less water would come out, but that's not the case. When you restrict the water, the same amount shoots out, but because it's under so much more pressure, it shoots out fifteen or twenty feet. It goes many times farther than it did with no pressure. In the same way, when the enemy puts you under pressure, he thinks it's going to stop you. What he doesn't realize is that all that pressure is going to cause you to shoot out further. When you feel restricted, when you face opposition, don't be discouraged. Get ready to shoot out. Get ready for new levels. Get ready for promotion. That pressure is not going to stop you; it's going to increase you.

When Jesus was about to be crucified, He went to the Garden of Gethsemane, which literally means "the place of pressing." It was an olive grove. The only way to get the valuable oil out of the olives is to press them. If you're never put under pressure, if you never have to stretch your faith, endure,

> *The only way to get the valuable oil out of the olives is to press them.*

overcome, and persevere, you won't tap into the treasures God put on the inside. On a Friday, Jesus was nailed to the cross—incredible pressure. On Saturday, He was in the grave, fighting the forces of darkness—restricted. But on Sunday morning, He came shooting up out of that grave. Death couldn't hold Him down. One message of the resurrection is that God uses our enemies to bless us.

Maybe you feel restricted today, pressured, as though you're being squeezed. It's Friday. Don't worry. Sunday is coming. The pressure is going to cause you to shoot out. When you see where God takes you—the favor, the blessing, the promotion—you're going to look back and say, as the psalmist said, "It was good that I was afflicted." David would tell you that it was good that Goliath showed up. Jesus would say that it was good that Judas betrayed Him. I can tell you that it was good that executive was against us, and it was good that coach said I was too small. The Israelites would tell you that it was good that Pharaoh restricted them. It may not have been comfortable at the time, but one day you will say, "That enemy didn't defeat me; that enemy blessed me." Now stay in faith, for God has your back. He wouldn't allow the pressure if it weren't going to work for your good. It may be Friday in your life, but Sunday is coming. You're about to shoot out, stronger, healthier, promoted, vindicated, and better off than you were before.

CHAPTER SEVEN

It's All Good

Life is full of things that we don't like—we get disappointed, a friend betrays us, we didn't get the promotion that we worked so hard for. We see these things as being negative, thinking, *That was bad. It didn't work out. My prayers didn't get answered.* It's easy to get discouraged and lose our passion. But God won't allow a difficulty unless He's going to somehow use it for our good. You may not understand how He's going to do it, but if you'll keep the right attitude, everything that happens in life will push you further into your destiny. This includes the closed doors you face, the delays, the person who did you wrong, and the loan that didn't go through. God says, "It's all good. I'm in control. It may not feel good, but if you'll trust Me, I'm going to use it for your good."

When you understand this principle, life gets much more freeing. You don't get upset when a coworker plays politics and leaves you out. You know it's all good. God allowed it, and He's going to use it. You tried, and the business didn't make it. You don't give up on your dreams. You know it's all good. It's a part of the process. You don't let simple things, such as getting stuck in traffic, get you frustrated and ruin your day. You know that God is directing your steps. By slowing you down, He may be keeping you from an accident. He may be developing patience in you. Whatever it is, He has a purpose for it. Keep the right perspective: it's all good.

This boils down to trusting God. We're not going to understand everything that happens and doesn't happen in our lives. If you try to figure it all out, you'll get frustrated. God can see the big picture for our lives. He knows where the dead ends are, the shortcuts, the bumpy roads that are going to cause you heartache and pain. He'll keep doors closed that you prayed would open, because He knows going through them would be a waste of your time. When you're mature, instead of getting

> *He knows where the dead ends are, the shortcuts, the bumpy roads that are going to cause you heartache and pain.*

bitter when things don't work out, you'll say, "God, I trust You. I may not like it, but I believe You know what's best for me."

All Things Work Together for Good

Some of the things that God has in your future you wouldn't be able to handle if He gave them to you right now. He loves you too much to let that happen. He's developing your character, growing you up. That boss who gets on your nerves, who doesn't treat you right—you keep trying to pray him away. The reason he's not going away is that God is using him like sandpaper to rub the rough edges off you. As you keep doing the right thing, keeping your mouth closed, being respectful, being faithful to your responsibilities, that's doing a work in you. You couldn't develop your character without him. You may not like it, but it's good. It's getting you ready for the next level of your destiny. God is asking, "Do you trust Me with your closed doors? Do you trust Me with your unanswered prayers, with the things you don't understand?"

Why don't you quit fighting everything you don't like and have this new perspective: it's all good? "I can't stand my grouchy boss, but I know he's good for me." This could be your perspective on a child who's hard to raise, an illness you're dealing with, or a dream that's taking forever to be fulfilled. You can say, "I don't like how this has gone, but I'm not going to live bitter. I know that God is on the throne, and He's in control of my life. This thing that has come against me may have been meant to harm me, but He promised He would use it to my advantage." This is what the apostle Paul said in Romans 8:28: "All things work together for good for those who love God." He did not say some things, but *all things*. They may not be good at the time we go through them. It's painful to go through a loss. It hurts when people do us wrong. It's discouraging when a dream doesn't work out. By themselves, they may not be good, but God promises He's going to bring it all together. One day you'll look back and say that it was all good.

"Well, Joel, I'm discouraged because I lost a loved one. I'm bitter because a business partner cheated me. Those things weren't good." When you say that, the problem is that you're isolating single incidents. God hasn't brought them together yet. If that bad break were going to keep you from your destiny, God wouldn't have allowed it. That setback was a

> *When you have this attitude that it's all good, you don't go around with a chip on your shoulder.*

setup for God to show out in your life. You have to get rid of the victim mentality and start having a victor mentality. When you have this attitude that it's all good, you don't go around with a chip on your shoulder. You know God has you in the palms of His hands. You have a spring in your step and a smile on your face, because you know it's just a matter of time before God brings it all together. Scripture says that weeping may endure for a night, but joy comes in the morning.

Good Friday May Not Feel Good

We celebrate Good Friday each year. We call it "good" now, but two thousand years ago, on the day when Jesus was crucified, it didn't look like a good Friday. The disciples thought it was the worst day of their lives. Their dreams were shattered. The Man Whom they had devoted their lives to had been crucified, was dead, and had been buried in a tomb. Doubts filled their minds: *Maybe He wasn't Who He said He was. Maybe He tricked us, and we wasted all that time.* You can imagine Mary, the mother of Christ, weeping as she watched her Son hanging on the cross. She was heartbroken, in so much pain. If someone had suggested, "Mary, this is a good Friday," she would have thought they had lost their mind. "What do you mean, this is good? Look at what's happening." We all face times when life doesn't make sense. A dream dies, a relationship ends, we come down with an illness—nothing about the situation seems good. *Good* is the last word we would have used to describe that Friday if we had been there. *Tragic Friday, betrayed Friday, lonely Friday* would have seemed like more accurate descriptions.

When you're in the heat of the battle, it's easy to get discouraged. The disciples could have said, "God, why did You let Judas betray Him? Why did You let the soldiers crucify Him? Why did You abandon Him in His time of greatest need?" But a few days later, when Jesus rose from the dead and appeared to them in the upper room and later cooked them breakfast on a beach, they realized that He was Who He'd said He was. He had done what He'd said He was going to do. He'd defeated the enemy and brought salvation to mankind. They looked back on that Friday and said, "It wasn't what we thought. It wasn't depressing Friday; it wasn't tragic Friday. It was all a part of His plan. It was Good Friday." When they looked

> *When they looked back, what they'd thought was the worst day of their lives they now called "good."*

back, what they'd thought was the worst day of their lives they now called "good."

What am I saying? It's all good. It may not be good right now, and it may not make sense on its own, but God knows how to bring it all together. You may think it is going to stop you, set you back, and cause you heartache. If you'll stay in faith, one day you'll look back and say it was good.

God Will Bring It All Together

When God brings it all together, when you meet the divine connection He has for you, somebody better than you ever dreamed, you'll look back and say with a smile, "It was a good Friday when that other person walked away!" Or what about the supervisor who tried to keep you down all those years? You didn't realize it at the time, but staying in that workplace with a good attitude, giving your best, and doing the right thing when the wrong thing was happening was developing your character, strengthening your spiritual muscles, getting you prepared for the next level. You wouldn't be who you are without that difficulty. You didn't like it at the time, but you look back now and say that was a good Friday.

That's what happened to us. Twice we tried to

buy property for a new sanctuary, and both times the property was sold out from under us. I was so disappointed. With the first property, we had worked on the deal for about six months, doing soil samples and preliminary drawings. When we walked into the office to sign the contract that morning, the secretary came out and announced that the owner had sold the property on the previous evening. It had been on the market for over twenty years! I came home disappointed and told Victoria there was no more property for us to build on. I didn't see anything good about somebody's not keeping their word to sell us that property. If you had told me it was a good Friday, I would have told you that you weren't thinking clearly.

A few months later, we found another hundred-acre tract of land. We thought this was even better than the first property. I prayed, "God, please open this door. Lord, thank You that we have Your favor." But the same thing happened. They sold the property to someone else. It didn't make sense to me. But I've learned that God's ways are better than our ways. The right way to pray is by saying, "God, this is what I want. This is what I'm believing for, but God, You know what's best for me. I trust You."

About six months after that second property was sold out from under us, we received word that the former Compaq Center was coming available. I realize now that the reason God closed those other doors is that He had something much better in store for us. God can see things that we can't see. Now I thank Him for closing those doors. I

I realize now that the reason God closed those other doors is that He had something much better in store for us.

look back and say, "That wasn't a defeated Friday after all. That was a good Friday." That was God keeping me from receiving less than He had in store for us. Sometimes God closes doors because we're believing too small. You may have dreams that haven't worked out yet; you've had some disappointed Fridays. Don't get discouraged. God knows what He's doing. If you'll keep honoring Him, being your best, then your Sunday is coming. God will open doors that no man can shut.

Open Doors, Closed Doors

My father went through a great disappointment. He had pastored a church for many years and given his heart and soul to help the people. They had just built a beautiful new sanctuary, the church was growing, and he was on the state board for his denomination. Life was good. It looked as though his future was very bright. But my sister Lisa was born with a condition similar to cerebral palsy. He began to read the Bible with a fresh set of eyes. He saw how God healed people and how we're supposed to live a victorious, abundant life. He started sharing this with his congregation. Much to his surprise, they didn't like his new message. It didn't fit into their denominational teaching, and he ended up having to leave the church. My mother had lifelong friends who never spoke to her again. My father and mother felt betrayed and discouraged. It didn't seem as though there was anything good about having to leave a position that he had worked so hard for. It felt like a dark Friday, a defeated Friday, a betrayed Friday to leave the people they had grown to love and care for.

But just as God opens doors, He closes doors. God knew that if my father stayed in that limited environment, he would never become who he was created to be. We love open doors because we know they are signs of God's favor. But when God closes a door, it takes maturity to say, "I don't understand it, but I'm not going to get bitter, and I'm not going to fight it. God, I trust You." Instead of sitting around in self-pity, thinking about what didn't work out and what was taken away, my parents went out and started Lakewood Church in a small run-down feed store with ninety people. It grew and grew to a church of thousands, and we're still going strong today. Looking back years later, my father would have told you, "That betrayal, getting pushed out, that was a good Friday." That was one of the best things that could have happened to him. It pushed him to a new level of his destiny. But at that time, it didn't look or feel good.

When you're hurting and disappointed, every thought tells you, "It's not fair, God. Why did You let this happen to me?" I'm asking you to trust Him. God knows what He's doing. It may not seem good, but one day when God brings it all together, you'll look back and say, "It was a good Friday." I couldn't see it at the time, but it was good when they sold the properties out from under us. Jesus would say it was good when Judas betrayed Him. My father would tell you it was good when they pushed him out of his position.

You may be in a Friday right now—nothing seems good about your situation. You're dealing with an illness, or struggling in a relationship, or have people coming against you. It feels dark, lonely, discouraging. You don't see how it could ever work out. Stay in faith. God wouldn't have allowed it if it weren't going to move

You're in Friday; the good news is that Sunday is coming, when you'll see your resurrection, so to speak.

you forward. You're in Friday; the good news is that Sunday is coming, when you'll see your resurrection, so to speak. Sunday is when God vindicates you, heals you, promotes you, restores you. It's when He prepares a table for you in the presence of your enemies, when He pays you back double for that difficulty. That's what turns defeated Friday into good Friday. No more betrayed Friday, disappointed Friday. Now it's blessed Friday, joyful Friday, victorious Friday.

It's Not All about Us

A couple would go up to the hospital every week to encourage the patients. One day the man had just parked his car and was walking across the street to the hospital's main entrance. A speeding car came around the corner, almost out of control, and hit the man. It knocked him up onto the hood, over the car, and onto the pavement. They rushed him to the emergency room and discovered that he had bleeding in his brain. They took a full-body scan to see if anything else was injured, looking for broken bones or any other bleeding. That was all fine, but they noticed a tumor on his kidney. When they did a biopsy, they found it was cancer. A few days after the bleeding stopped, he had surgery to remove the kidney. Everything went fine, and today he is cancer-free. The doctor told him that if they had not found that tumor, there was a good chance the cancer would have spread to other parts of his body and become life-threatening.

Friend, it's all good—even things that at the time seem bad, such as getting hit by a car when you're doing a good deed. Most people would say, "Boy, you're unlucky. Too bad for you." But God doesn't allow anything out of which He can't bring good. We don't always see it. "Joel, I've had a bunch of things happen to me that did nothing but pull me down." You don't know what God is doing behind the scenes. It may not have all come together yet. This is what faith is all about. When things happen that we don't like—disappointments, betrayals, bad breaks—we can get negative and live bitter. Or we can say, "God, I trust You. You know what's best for me. Even when I don't understand it, I believe that when it comes together, it's going to work for me and not against me."

Two young college students were traveling to Kenya to work on a mission project. They were in their early twenties, both former college basketball players. This was their first trip overseas. They had prayed that everything would go smoothly. But when the plane tried to land in London, it was delayed by a heavy fog, and they missed their connecting flight. They were disappointed, thinking what a poor way this was for their trip to get started. They had to spend the night trying to sleep in the airport. The only seats available on the next flight were in first class, so they were put right up front. About midway through the flight, without warning the plane took a nosedive and started heading straight toward the ground. People were panicking and screaming. It looked as though they were going to die. These young men heard noise in the cockpit that sounded like a struggle. This was before the 9/11 attacks, when the doors into the cockpit were not locked. They opened the cockpit door and found a deranged man had gotten into the cabin and taken over the controls of the plane. The pilots were trying to pull him off, but they were very small men and couldn't budge him. Both of these young men were over six foot six, big and strong. They grabbed that man, ripped him off the controls, and tied him up. The plane had descended from thirty thousand feet to four thousand feet. Another minute or two, and everyone on that flight would have been killed.

That fog delay and missed connection seemed like a bad thing, but really it was good. The young men couldn't see it at the time. They didn't like it. Sleeping in the airport didn't fit into their plans. But God held them back on purpose so they could save the plane and its passengers. Sometimes God will inconvenience you in order to help somebody else. Instead of getting frustrated when our plans don't work out, we need to remember it's not all about us. "I don't like my job. The people are negative, they gossip, they compromise. When is God going to move me out?" Maybe God has you there on purpose to let your light shine. Maybe He's counting on you to be a good influence on them. Quit fighting everything you don't like. The psalmist said, "The steps of a good person are ordered by the Lord." If God has you there, He's ordered your steps. You may not like the delays, the inconveniences, and the unfair situations. It may be uncomfortable, but instead of resisting it, trying to pray it away, why don't you embrace it? Say, "God, this is where You have me right now, so I'm going to be my best. I'm going to have a good attitude. I may not like it, it may feel bad, but I know a secret: it's all good." It's not working against you; it's working for you.

> *Instead of getting frustrated when our plans don't work out, we need to remember it's not all about us.*

What You Don't See

Quit fighting everything you don't like. Quit being upset because you had a bad break, went through a disappointment, got a medical report that wasn't what you'd hoped for. God wouldn't allow it if it weren't going to work for your good. It looks like a setback, but really it's a setup to move you into your destiny.

Remember that after Joseph endured thirteen years of betrayals, disappointments, and lonely nights with a good attitude in an Egyptian prison, he was made the second-most powerful person in Egypt. Despite what he went through, he would have told you exactly what he later told his brothers who had sold him into slavery: it was all good. It was all a part of the plan. My friends Craig and Samantha, whom I introduced in the previous chapter, didn't understand having a child with autism, but now after starting the Champions Club and helping so many other parents with special needs children, they would tell you it was all good.

You may not see it right now, but there's a blessing in the darkness. When it all comes together, it's going to work to your advantage. It may be Friday in your life, with no reason to call what you're going through good, but don't worry, because Sunday is coming. God is still on the throne. If you'll stay in faith, everything that was meant to stop you, God is going to use to push you forward. He's bringing it all together right now. Good Friday is coming. Blessed Friday, vindicated Friday, healthy Friday, victorious Friday is headed your way!

You may not see it right now, but there's a blessing in the darkness.

CHAPTER EIGHT

Nothing Is Wasted

Victoria and I have some flower beds at home, and several times a year we'll put mulch in those beds. The mulch we use is a fertilizer that helps the plants grow. One of the main ingredients of the mulch is manure. It's waste, and it smells really bad. For several days after we apply it, we can hardly stand to walk outside the house. My kids say, "Dad, what happened? It stinks out here." But if you come back in a month or two, the smell is gone and the plants are blooming, blossoming, filled out with lots of new growth. That fertilizer, as bad as it smells, is giving the plants valuable nutrients and minerals that they could not get on their own.

In a similar way, we all go through things in life that stink. We don't like what has happened; something wasn't fair. "Why did this person do me wrong?" "Why did our relationship not make it?" "Why did I come down with this sickness?" "Why did I lose my main client? This stinks." You need to have a new perspective: that's just fertilizer. It may smell bad right now. It seems as though a pile of manure got dumped on you. You could easily be discouraged, but if you'll stay in faith, it's not going to hinder you; it's going to strengthen you, it's going to develop you. The stinky stuff—the betrayal, the disappointment, the loss—is getting you prepared for new growth, to bloom, to blossom, to become all you were created to be.

The truth is, you cannot reach your highest potential without fertilizer. The stinky stuff is not working against you; it's working for you. It may smell bad for a little while, but if you'll keep doing the right thing, you'll come into a new season of growth and opportunities for new levels of your destiny. I'd love to tell you that if you'll just trust God and be your best, you'll sail through life with no difficulties, but that's not reality. You're going to have some manure. There's going to be some smelly stuff coming your way. What I want you to see is that it's not working

> *The truth is, you cannot reach your highest potential without fertilizer.*

against you; it's working for you. Instead of getting depressed and thinking, *This stinks. I can't believe this happened*, have this attitude: *It's just more fertilizer. God's getting me prepared for something greater.* If you'll go through the stink with the right attitude and not let it sour your life, God will take what was meant for your harm and use it for your good.

You may feel as though you've already had more than your share of stinky stuff—bad breaks, disappointments, broken dreams. Be encouraged, because that means you have a lot of fertilizer. God is getting you ready to go where you've never been. This is not the time to feel sorry for yourself and live with a chip on your shoulder, thinking about all you've been through. This is the time to get ready. God allowed that fertilizer to get you prepared for where you could not go on your own. You may not have liked it, but it deposited something on the inside that you could only get by going through it. Quit complaining about the fertilizer—about who hurt you and what didn't work out—and all the manure that got dumped on you. Without the fertilizer, without the smelly stuff, you couldn't reach your destiny. It's not hindering you; it's helping you. If it were too much, God wouldn't have allowed it. You have to dig your heels in and say, "I am in it to win it. I'm not going to let this stinky stuff, this manure, this stuff I don't understand, cause me to get sour and give up on my dreams. I may not like it, but I know it's fertilizer. It's enriching me. It's making me stronger. It's getting me prepared for new levels."

Let Life's Fertilizers Work

There was a young lady who grew up in a very difficult environment. Her father died when she was six years old, and shortly after that her mother had to go on dialysis. When other kids her age were involved in cheerleading and out playing with their friends, she was at home taking care of her mother, helping run the kidney machine. At twelve years old, she had to go grocery shopping and cook for the family. She got her little brother dressed and ready for school each day. It seemed she was at a disadvantage, that this hardship would put her behind and keep her from her destiny. But just because something is unfair doesn't mean that God doesn't still have an amazing future in front in you. It may stink, but remember that manure has a lot of helpful ingredients; manure is fertilizer. People spend a lot of money to have manure put in their flower beds. It seems as though it's a waste, but used in the right way, it's an advantage. It causes growth.

This young lady didn't have a victim mentality; she had a victor mentality. It was hard, and it wasn't fair, but she didn't complain or feel sorry for herself. She just kept being her best, shaking off the self-pity, not letting negative thoughts talk her out of her dreams. Despite all the odds stacked against her, she excelled in high school and received a full scholarship to a major university. She went on to get her master's, and then she earned a doctorate degree. Today she's extremely successful in the corporate world and happily married with three beautiful children.

Here's my question: why do some people in that same type of situation struggle through life, living defeated, discouraged, and always overcome by problems, while others, such as her, overcome the odds, flourish, and see God's goodness in amazing ways? It's in how we approach life. We all have stinky stuff; we all have unfair situations, things we don't like. You can get bitter, discouraged, and sour, or you can see it as fertilizer and say, "This difficulty is not going to defeat me; it's going to promote me. It's not going to hinder me; it's going to help me." God wouldn't have allowed it unless He had a purpose. Don't just go through it, grow through it. Recognize that it's making you stronger. You're developing character, perseverance, trust, and confidence.

A difficult, dark time in your life doesn't have to keep you from your destiny. Actually, it can do just the opposite. It can propel you into your destiny. What stinks in your life right now, and what you don't like, can be the very thing that promotes you and causes you to blossom. Without the fertilizer, you couldn't reach your highest potential. Don't complain about the stink; there's promotion in that stink. Don't get sour because of the smelly stuff; there's a new level in that smelly stuff. Don't be discouraged by the manure. You may not like it, but that's fertilizer. That's what gets you prepared for the great future God has in store. You may feel as though you got too much fertilizer. But if you got a lot of stinky things that you could complain about, it's because God has a big destiny in front of you. He's going to take you somewhere you've never dreamed of. He's getting you prepared for blessings. Your roots are going down deeper. The manure doesn't smell good, but it has nutrients and minerals; it's making you stronger.

> *What stinks in your life right now, and what you don't like, can be the very thing that promotes you and causes you to blossom.*

The next time you see that person at work who gets on your nerves and doesn't treat you with respect, instead of getting upset, just smile and say to yourself, "You're just fertilizer. You stink, but you're helping me grow. You think you're pushing me down, but really you're pushing me up." When you go through a disappointment or a setback, or the medical report isn't good, you can be honest and say, "This stinks. I don't like it, but I know a secret. It's just fertilizer. It's going to cause me to bloom, to blossom, to flourish."

From the Pit to the Prison to the Palace

This is what Joseph did. His brothers were jealous of him and threw him into a pit. He could have gotten depressed and said, "God, I don't understand this. I'm a good person." Instead he realized, "It's just fertilizer. They're trying to stop me, but God's going to use it to increase me." However, that was just the beginning. One bad thing after another happened to Joseph after that. His brothers sold him into slavery in Egypt, where his master's wife lied about him, falsely accused him of a crime, and had him thrown into prison. He spent thirteen years there for something he didn't do. They were trying to hold him down, but they didn't realize they were pouring fertilizer on him. Joseph kept growing, getting stronger, his roots going down deeper in faith. They thought they were stopping him, but the truth is, they were strengthening him. All that injustice, that stinky stuff, seemed like a waste of years of his life, but just as fertilizer feeds a plant nutrients and minerals, that difficult, dark season was doing a work in Joseph, getting him prepared for the fullness of his destiny.

If you'll stay in faith in the stinky times, the times that don't make sense, when you're not treated fairly, when you're doing the right thing but the wrong things keep happening, your time will come to bloom, to be promoted, to be blessed, to be vindicated, and all the forces of darkness cannot stop you. People don't have the final say; God has the final say. He will get you to where you're supposed to be.

Joseph went from the pit to the prison and all the way to the palace. You may feel that you're in the pits right now. Perhaps you've had some bad breaks, you're dealing with a sickness, you've lost a loved one, a friend betrayed you, a dream died. But as was true of Joseph, that pit is not the end of your story, and the prison is not your final chapter. Your destiny is the palace. God destined you to live a victorious life. David said, "God lifted me out of a hor-

> *Joseph went from the pit to the prison and all the way to the palace.*

rible pit and put a new song in my mouth." You may be in the pit, but you need to get ready, because you're coming out. That depression is not the end. That sickness is not the end, and that addiction is not the final chapter. The person who walked out on you and did you wrong is not the end. If they left you, you didn't need them. If they walked out, they were not a part of your destiny. God has somebody better. He wants to put a new song in your heart. Don't get comfortable in the pit. Don't let self-pity and discouragement steal your passion. You have to get your fire back. Every blessing that God promised you He still has every intention of bringing to pass. The palace is in your future. Victory is in your future. Dreams coming to pass are in your future, with increase, abundance, promotion, health, and restoration. That's what's up in front of you. That's where your story ends.

I talked to a man who was very upset because his boss was against him and always trying to make him look bad. This boss was jealous of him, and he went out of his way not to give the man any recognition. I told him, "It's just fertilizer. Stay on the high road, and God will not only do a work in you, but He'll take care of your enemies. It may stink right now, but don't worry—fertilizer stinks. That means you're about to see new growth." This man got his passion back and went to the office being his best, taking the high road, working as unto God, not unto man. On several occasions he should have been promoted, but because of this unfair boss's tainted views, he was passed over. One day the CEO of the whole company was in town, and this man had to give a report. The CEO was very impressed with his work. About a year later, a position became available that would normally have gone to his boss, but the CEO skipped over the boss and went straight to this man and offered him the position. Now instead of his having to work for the boss who was hard to get along with, the tables have turned, and the boss is working for him! One touch of God's favor and you'll go from the back to the front, from the employee to the employer, from the pit to the palace.

We all have some stinky stuff, things that are not fair, people who are not treating us right, situations we don't understand. You have to do as Joseph did and see it as fertilizer. It's not going to stop you; it's going to promote you. Don't get upset with the person who lied about you and tried to make you look bad. They just spread some fertilizer on you. They thought they were pushing you down, but in reality they were pushing you up. You're one step closer to your palace.

No Experience Is Wasted

Perhaps because of a mistake you made, you feel as though you're all washed up and have blown your chance. Remember that God uses the stinky stuff. You can't blossom into all you were created to be without some smelly stuff. It's not working against you; it's working for you. Sometimes we do bring trouble on ourselves. We make poor decisions, and the accuser whispers in our ear, "You don't deserve to be blessed. It's your fault. God's not going to help you." But God doesn't waste anything. He knows how to get good out of every situation. It may not be good, but He can cause it to work for our good.

In John 4, Jesus met a woman at a well outside a city in Samaria, and He told her that He would give her "living water." She said, "Please, give me this water." He replied, "Go, call your husband." She responded, "I don't have a husband." Jesus said, "You're right, for you've had five husbands, and the one whom you're living with is not your husband." She was amazed that this stranger could know everything about her. She said to Jesus, "I know one day the Messiah is coming." Jesus answered her, "I am the Messiah." The first person Jesus ever told that He was the Messiah was this woman—a woman who had a rough past, had made many mistakes, and had gone through some stinky situations. She went back into the city and told the whole town, "Come and see a man who told me everything I ever did. Could this be the Messiah?" God used her as the first evangelist to get the word out that He was the Messiah. Here's my point. Having been married five times, this woman was comfortable around men. If she had been easily intimidated and quiet, she wouldn't have told many people. God took what the enemy had used against her—her boldness, her straightforwardness—and turned it around and said in effect, "That's gotten you into trouble in the past, but I'm going to make the enemy pay. I'm going to use that to advance the kingdom." It had worked against her; now it was working for her.

God knows how to use what you've been through. He doesn't waste your experiences. You may have made poor choices, but He can turn your mess into your message. He'll use you to help others who are going through the same thing.

> *You may have made poor choices, but He can turn your mess into your message.*

A friend of mine spent several years in an outlaw motorcycle gang. He was on drugs, running with the wrong crowd, breaking the law, in and out of jail. It looked as though he would never change, but this young man had a praying mother. Every day this mother said, "God, You promised that my children will be mighty in the land. Thank You for turning my son around." One Sunday morning he was in such a dark place of depression and so high on drugs that he decided to end his life. Just as he was about to take a bottle of pills, for some reason he turned on the television, and there was my father ministering. This young man got on his motorcycle, still high on drugs, rode to Lakewood, and walked into the service—rough, leather jacket, tattoos, beard, mean as he could be. The usher brought him right down front to sit. That day he felt a love that he'd never felt. In the parking lot after the service, he got down on his knees in front of his motorcycle and said, "God, if You're real, help me to change. I'm giving my life to You." Today that man is a pastor of a church, and he has a motorcycle ministry. He goes back to the outlaw gang members and shares his story of how God changed his life. God doesn't waste any experience. He doesn't waste what you've been through. He'll use you to help others who are dealing with the same thing.

There was a story on the news about a twenty-year-old gunman who walked into an elementary school with an assault rifle and started shooting at police officers surrounding the building. Fortunately, he didn't hit anyone. After everyone scattered, he barricaded himself in a small room. Hiding behind the counter was the school accountant, a middle-aged lady named Ms. Tuff. She had the right name. She stood up, their eyes met, and he pointed the rifle. Rather than panic, she started talking to him. She's a very kind, gentle woman, as calm as can be. The young man was drawn to her, and he began to open up. He told her how he was off his medicine and felt hopeless, as though there were no purpose for his life. Ms. Tuff said, "I know how you feel. My husband left me after thirty-three years of marriage, and last year I tried to commit suicide, but by the grace of God it didn't happen" (my paraphrase from different news sources). She went on to tell him about how God had given her a new beginning, that her life had been restored, and about how she had opened a new business and was excited about her future. She said, "If God did it for me, He can do it for you." Standing there with the assault rifle, a SWAT team outside, students hiding in their classrooms, and helicopters overhead, the young man put the gun down and walked out peacefully, and nobody was harmed. She said afterward, "God put me there because I had been through what he was going through." Nothing is wasted—the good, the bad, the painful. God knows how to bring blessing out of the dark places. No matter what comes your way, if you'll stay in faith, not only will it act like fertilizer and help you, but down the road you'll be instrumental in helping others.

Making Music out of Trash

The Scripture records one of the times when David was on the run from King Saul, who was jealous of him and trying to kill him. David had left in such a hurry that he hadn't taken his sword. He got to the next city and told the local priest he was on assignment from the king, and it was so urgent he hadn't had time to get a weapon. He asked the priest if he had a sword or spear he could borrow. The man said, "All we have is the sword of Goliath, the Philistine whom you killed in the valley." David's face lit up. He said, "There's nothing like that sword. Let

The enemies that try to defeat you—the depression, the bad breaks, the sickness, the injustice—not only are you going to defeat them, but you will use those experiences to defeat others.

me have it." David left that day with the sword that had been meant to defeat him, and he used that same sword to defeat others. The enemies that try to defeat you—the depression, the bad breaks, the sickness, the injustice—not only are you going to defeat them, but you will use those experiences to defeat others. You have some swords for your future—things you've overcome, battles you've won, enemies you've defeated, challenges you've outlasted. Those victories will be there when you need them. It was meant for your harm, it was meant to stop you, it was meant to keep you from your destiny, but God knows how to not only turn it around, not only give you the victory, but put that sword in your future. That will help you overcome other obstacles.

I saw a report about a small city in South America that was built on a garbage dump. Trash is everywhere—in the streets, in the river, in their yards. All you can see is waste. Very poor people live there with little electricity or running water. They make their living by going through the trash, looking for anything they can sell. Hour after hour, they rummage through it to earn just a few cents a day. It didn't look as though anything good could come out of that dark place. But when a gentleman named Favio Chávez came to the city and saw the children playing in the trash, it broke his heart. He wanted to help. He decided to start a music school right there in the trash heap. He didn't have money for instruments, so he and a carpenter who lived in the town started looking through the trash for materials they could use to make instruments. Old pipe would be part of a saxophone, and discarded wood boxes became part of a guitar. Buckets and barrels of different sizes were used for drums. In a few months he had violins, cellos, guitars, and drums—all made out of trash.

Being a musician himself, Chávez taught the children how to play. They were very excited. Now they have what they call the Recycled Orchestra, made up of dozens of children who play the instruments made from the garbage heap. After they put a clip on YouTube and it went viral, they started getting invitations to play from around the world. Today they fill concert halls everywhere they go, playing before tens of thousands of people. People were so moved by what they saw and heard that they started donating not only new instruments but also funds to help the children. At the end of the report, reporters talked with a noted musician, who made a statement that stuck with me. She said, "I couldn't

He knows how to make music out of our mess.

believe you could make music with trash." That's what our God does. He can take the broken pieces of our lives—the mistakes, the injustices, what seems like a waste and looks like nothing good will ever come out of it—and He knows how to make music out of our mess. Other people may not be able to see it, but God can see it.

Rise to the Top

God has you in the palms of His hands. Nothing that's happened to you has been wasted. It's all a part of the plan to make you into who you were created to be. It may not have been good, but God can cause it to work out for your good. He can take the same thing that should have destroyed you and use it to propel you. No obstacle is too big, no challenge too great. The forces that are for you are greater than the forces that are against you.

You may be going through a tough time, as David did, but you're about to come into one of your swords. God is going to use what you've been through to catapult you forward. People can't stop it, bad breaks can't stop it, trash can't stop it, injustice can't stop it, and mistakes you've made don't have to stop it. Like Joseph, you're about to rise to the top. You may be in a dark pit, but the palace is coming. Let go of what didn't work out, shake off the self-pity, the doubt, and the discouragement, for this is a new day. God has new mountains for you to climb. Your best days are not your yesterdays; they are still out in front of you. The enemy wouldn't be fighting you this hard if he didn't know that God has something amazing in your future. It may be difficult, it may stink, but remember that it's fertilizer. It's working for you. You're growing, you're getting stronger. I believe and declare you're about to bloom, you're about to blossom, you're about to flourish. I speak victory over you, I speak restoration, and I speak new beginnings and blessings—health, wholeness, creativity, justice, vindication, abundance, the fullness of your destiny!

CHAPTER NINE

Trouble Is Transportation

We all go through difficulties in life, things we don't understand. It's easy to get discouraged and think, *Why is this happening to me?* But God uses difficulties to move us toward our destiny. Nothing happens by accident. You may not understand it, but God wouldn't have allowed it if it weren't going to work to your advantage. Looking back over my life, I see the importance of the times when I was most uncomfortable, when I went through a disappointment or somebody did me wrong. It didn't make sense to me then, but years later I realized that if it had not happened, I would never have met a certain person. If that door hadn't closed, this bigger door would never have opened. If those people hadn't done me wrong, I wouldn't have the experience that I need for this new challenge. Now I can see that the whole time, God was directing my steps. I thought I was going backward, but He was setting me up to move forward. I didn't like it, I felt stuck, but the truth is that trouble was transportation; it was moving me into my destiny.

You won't become all you were created to be without trouble. You don't grow in the good times; you grow in the tough times, the dark times. Trouble prepares you for the next level. Trouble develops something in you that you can't get when it's easy and everything is going your way. In the difficult times your spiritual muscles are developed, and you gain strength, endurance, and wisdom. Every challenge you've been through has deposited something in you. Through every relationship that didn't work out, you gained experience that will help you in the future. The times when you failed, when you blew it, weren't wasted—you gained insight. It was all a part of God's plan.

Quit complaining about the trouble. Quit being discouraged because life dealt you a tough hand. The reason you have big challenges is that you have a big destiny. Average people have average problems; ordinary people have ordinary challenges. You're not average; you're not ordinary. You're a child of the Most High God. The Creator of

You're not ordinary; you're extraordinary. Don't be surprised if you face extraordinary challenges.

the universe breathed His life into you. He crowned you with His favor. He put seeds of greatness on the inside. You're not ordinary; you're extraordinary. Don't be surprised if you face extraordinary challenges. It's because you have an extraordinary destiny. God is getting you prepared for greater blessings than you can imagine.

Trouble Moves You toward Your Destiny

Think about Moses. He was born into trouble that was no fault of his own. As a little baby, when he was most vulnerable, life dealt him an unfair hand. For fear of the increasing population of Israelites in Egypt, the Pharaoh ordered the midwives to kill all the male Hebrew babies. It looked as though Moses were done. Some would say that it was too bad he was born at the wrong time. But Moses' mother understood the principle we're discussing: she believed trouble couldn't keep her son from his destiny. When she could no longer safely hide him at home, she placed Moses in a papyrus basket and hid it among the reeds along the bank of the Nile River. Even though his sister was standing at a distance watching over him, there were snakes, alligators, and all kinds of natural dangers. The basket could have tipped over, and Moses could have drowned. If the wrong person had discovered him there, his sister could not have stopped that person from obeying Pharaoh's command to throw the Hebrew baby boy into the Nile. A thousand things could have ended Moses' life, but none of it was a surprise to God. Pharaoh's death decree didn't cancel Moses' purpose. God has the final say. People don't determine your destiny; God does.

It just so happened that of all people, Pharaoh's daughter, a princess, decided to go down to the river and take a bath. She saw his little basket floating among the reeds and sent her servant to get it. She opened the basket up, and there was baby Moses, who started crying. It was love at first sight. Even though she knew Moses was a Hebrew baby, she was so thrilled that she picked him up and said, "I'm going to take this baby as my own." And so Moses was raised in the palace of Pharaoh's daughter!

God could have stopped the trouble. He could have changed Pharaoh's mind and not allowed him to put out the dark decree that threatened Moses' life. But God used the trouble to get Moses to where He wanted him to be. The trouble was a part of God's plan. If Moses had been raised in the limited environment he'd been born into, he could not have learned what he needed to for his destiny. In the palace, under the Pharaoh, he learned the best of Egyptian civilization—about business, leadership, how to conduct a meeting, how to speak to people, and on and on. The Egyptians were known for their superior education and ingenuity. We still marvel at the colossal pyramids they built with no modern-day equipment.

But at the time that Moses was taken away from his home and family, I'm sure that Moses' mother couldn't understand it. It seemed like a setback, having to hide your baby in the river, and surely his sister must have thought it was the end when she saw Pharaoh's daughter opening the basket that day. But many years later, when God told Moses to go back to Egypt and tell the Pharaoh, "Let My people go," one of the reasons Moses could walk into Pharaoh's court with confidence was that he had lived in a palace and had been raised by royalty. He knew Egyptian protocol. He wasn't overwhelmed. He had grown up in that environment.

What was it that had prepared Moses to lead the Israelites out of Egypt? Trouble. It was being born in a dysfunctional situation, having the odds stacked against him. If Pharaoh had not put out the decree, Moses would have grown up in his own home, but as a slave with a limited education. God knows what

What was it that had prepared Moses to lead the Israelites out of Egypt? Trouble.

He's doing. You may not like the trouble, it may not be fair, you're uncomfortable, but that trouble is transportation. As it did for Moses, trouble is taking you to the next level of your destiny. It's getting you prepared. You wouldn't be who you are today without all the things you've been through.

When Backward Means Forward

The Scripture says that God didn't lead the Israelites on the easiest route to the Promised Land because they were not ready for war. He had to toughen them up so they would be prepared for what He had in store. Don't get discouraged by the trouble and say, "God, why is this happening to me?" That trouble is not going to defeat you; it's going to promote you. It's not hindering you; it's preparing you. You may not see how it could work out, but God has a way through the darkness. He's already lined up the right people. As He had for Moses, He has a Pharaoh's daughter who will be there to be good to you. He has the breaks you need, the vindication, the funds, and the healing. You trust God when everything is good, so why don't you trust Him in the times of trouble? Why don't you believe that even though you don't understand it, He's still directing your steps? You don't have to live feeling stressed out because you had a bad break or discouraged because you went through a disappointment. That trouble means you're on the way to your destiny. If you'll stay in faith, you'll see God begin to connect the dots. You'll see there was a reason that door closed and a reason you didn't get that promotion. God had something better in store. He was using that trouble to move you into your destiny.

I heard about a young man who grew up in Detroit through the 1930s and 1940s. His parents had immigrated to the United States from the small European country of Macedonia and didn't speak English. This young man loved playing baseball. His dream was to one day play for the Detroit Tigers. He was a great player all through high school, very talented. After high school he went away and served in the military. When he came back to Detroit in 1952, the Tigers offered him a four-year contract to play in their minor leagues. He was thrilled, worked hard, and kept getting better and better, believing that one day he would make it up to the big league. But three years into his career, he suffered a major knee injury and was forced to quit playing. He was very disappointed. Everything he had worked so hard for suddenly came to an end. He had to move back in with his parents. His father had warned him that he would never make it playing baseball. He couldn't live at home unless he got a job so he could help pay the rent.

This young man had a friend who owned a restaurant. He asked his friend if he could come work for him until he found another job. He said, "You don't even have to pay me. I just need somewhere to go each day so my father will know I'm working." He was going to pay his father with money he had saved from playing baseball. His friend said, "We don't have any job openings, but if you want to go in the back and help them make pizzas, you can." He started working in the restaurant for free, making pizzas. He got so good at making pizzas that he started his own pizza restaurant. People loved his pizza, and his restaurant was so successful that he opened another one and another and another. Today most of us have enjoyed a slice of pizza from Little Caesars, the restaurant he started. Yes, that knee injury was a big disappointment, but it wasn't the end. It was transportation; it moved him toward his destiny.

"Well, Joel, something like that would never happen for me." How do you know? Your story is not over. God is not finished with you. That bad break, that disappointment, that divorce is not your final chapter. If you'll do as he did and keep being your best, keep believing, keep praying, keep honoring God, then trouble won't be the end; it will be transportation. It will move you toward the new thing God has in store.

This man's dream of playing for the Detroit Tigers never came to pass, but today he owns the Detroit Tigers! For my friend Mike Ilitch, it didn't work out his way, but God had a better way. What you're dreaming about may be too small. That door may have closed because God has something bigger for you. You're working for

> *This man's dream of playing for the Detroit Tigers never came to pass, but today he owns the Detroit Tigers!*

a company, but one day you're going to own your own company. You're believing to manage that addiction, but God is going to free you from that addiction. You're thinking you'll be single for the rest of your life, but God is going to bring somebody to you who is better than you imagined. Don't get discouraged by the trouble; it's not the end. We trust God in the good times. I'm asking you to trust Him in the troubled times—when you don't understand what's going on and when you're uncomfortable. Dare to believe that He's in control, that He knows what's best, that your steps and your stops are ordered by the Lord. It's a powerful attitude when you can say, "God, I trust You in trouble. I trust You when it's not happening my way. I trust You even though I feel as though I'm going backward."

Strength, Power, and Grace to Go Through

A lot of times we're trying to pray away all our troubles, pray away the challenges, pray away the bad breaks. But here's the key: you're not anointed from trouble, you are anointed for trouble. The

You're not anointed from trouble, you are anointed for trouble.

Scripture says, "God is a present help in trouble." He is not going to stop every difficulty and every bad break, but He will give you the strength, the power, and the grace to go through the dark times with a good attitude. Psalm 89 says, "I have anointed David. I will steady him and make him strong. His enemies will not get the best of him. I will push down his adversaries and defeat his haters. He will rise to power because of Me." It doesn't say, "I will anoint him so he doesn't have any opposition or problems." It says, "I'm anointing him for the trouble, for the sickness, for the legal problem."

Quit telling yourself, "I can't take this! It's too much." You're anointed for that difficulty. "Well, I didn't get the promotion, the loan didn't go through, and my child got off course. That's why I'm discouraged." Have a new perspective. Right now, God is breathing in your direction, making you steady and strong. You don't have to fight those battles or live feeling stressed out because it's not happening your way. God said He will push down your adversaries. He will defeat your enemies. That sickness, that legal problem, that trouble at work will not get the best of you. Why? Because you're anointed for trouble. You are powerful, determined, favored. The Most High God says you're not going to stay in trouble. You will rise to power. That means you will see increase, promotion, healing, and blessing. You may be in trouble now, but don't worry—it's transportation that's moving you to the next level of your destiny. You're going to see God begin to connect the dots in your life. It may not make sense now, but one day you're going to look back and see what God was doing in the darkness. Even for the things you don't understand, if you'll keep the right attitude, you'll be able to say, "They made me stronger. I'm more determined. I developed a greater confidence."

A couple of years after Victoria and I were married, we sold a house and moved to a different place. Three months later, there was a knock on our door. I answered it, and a police officer was standing there. He handed me an envelope and said, "Somebody must not like you." The people who had bought our house were suing us over the plumbing. They also sued the builder, the architect, the Realtor, the plumber—about a dozen of us. We hadn't done anything wrong. We knew we weren't at fault. But I was twenty-five years old and had never dreamed I would be involved in a lawsuit. I didn't like it. I had to go downtown to the courthouse and give my deposition. I was so nervous and worried that afterward I couldn't drive home. Someone had to come pick me up. A few months later, the lawsuit was dropped and everything was fine. It seemed as though that whole ordeal, having to testify and go through the process, had been a waste of time and money. I didn't think any good would ever come out of it.

But sixteen years later, when we acquired the Compaq Center, a company filed a lawsuit to try to keep us from moving in. This time when I went to give my deposition, I wasn't the least bit nervous. I knew what to expect. I was confident, strong, and clear. Now I realize that God had allowed the lawsuit over the plumbing because He knew that sixteen years later there was going to be a lawsuit that mattered, that would affect my destiny. He had to get me prepared. I couldn't see it at the time, but I realize now that trouble was transportation. Instead of being upset when things come against you, why don't you believe that God knows what He's doing? Instead of living sour and complaining, "God, why is this happening?" have this perspective: "God, I know You have me in the palms of Your hands. I know You're directing my steps. Even when I don't understand it, I trust You."

Every Step Divinely Orchestrated

I wrote about Joseph in the previous chapter. When he was a teenager, God gave him a dream that he was destined for greatness, but before that dream came true, he went through a series of very dark places. There were many years when he did the right thing but the wrong thing happened. It didn't seem as though the dream would ever work out, but Joseph understood this principle: as he kept being his best, the trouble couldn't stop him—it was moving him toward his destiny. When you study his life, you can see how God connected the dots. Every step was divinely orchestrated. If you left one step out, the others wouldn't work. If Joseph's brothers had not thrown him into the pit, he would have never been taken to Egypt as a slave and sold to a man named Potiphar. If he had never been sold to Potiphar, he would never have met Potiphar's wife, been falsely accused, and put in prison. If he had not been put in prison, he would never have met the butler and the baker and interpreted their dreams. If he'd never interpreted their dreams, Pharaoh would never have called on him to interpret his dream, which led him to put Joseph in charge of the nation.

If you isolate any of those steps along the way, they don't make sense. It was just one bad break after another. But you have to believe, as Joseph did, that what looks like a disappointment, a betrayal, or a setback is all a part of God's plan. It's transportation. It's moving you little by little through the darkness into your destiny. God knows what He's doing. God knew that He was going to need somebody in charge in Egypt who would show favor to the Israelites. So years earlier, He'd started this plan to move Joseph into place. What looked like trouble was really the hand of God. Joseph's brothers took away his coat of many colors, which represented their father's favor, but they could not take away the calling on his life. What people

> *What looked like trouble was really the hand of God.*

take from you doesn't stop your purpose. What's on the inside is more powerful than anything on the outside. You keep doing the right thing despite the trouble, despite the betrayal, despite the bad break, and one day God is going to connect the dots for you just as He did for Joseph. He's going to take you to your throne, so to speak. You'll say, as Joseph said, "They meant the trouble for harm, but God used it for my good."

The Scripture says, "God will deliver us from trouble." That means that God will stop the trouble. But consider it in different light. The post office picks up a package in New York, and drivers deliver it to California. *Deliver* means they transport it; they move it from one location to another. It may have to go through five different stops along the way. The regional post office sends it to the city post office, which sends it to the neighborhood post office, and the mailman brings it to your house. It is *delivered*. In the same way, right now God is delivering you from trouble. You're en route, the process has started, and there may be some stops along the way. But don't worry, you're not delivered yet. Like Joseph, you may be in a pit or in the prison, but the palace is coming. You're in debt, but God is delivering you into abundance. You're dealing with depression, but God is delivering you into joy. You're facing an illness, but God is delivering you into healing, wholeness, and victory. When those thoughts tell you, "This trouble is permanent. It's never going to change," just answer back, "No, I'm being delivered. I'm en route. This trouble is not going to stop me; it's going to transport me."

Let the Journey Begin

I met a young lady named Victoria Arlen who grew up as a healthy child, very active, but when she was eleven years old had a pain in her side that wouldn't go away. The doctors took out her appendix, but that didn't help. Then her health started going downhill quickly. She lost thirty pounds in a few weeks. The doctors couldn't figure out what was wrong. Her legs started getting weak, she lost all movement in her arms, she couldn't swallow her food, and when she tried to speak, her words weren't there. Victoria described it as someone shutting off all the switches that controlled her body and her brain, until the lights went out. She ended up in the hospital in a vegetative state. She was unable to move, to open her eyes, or to communicate in any way—she was gone. The doctors finally diagnosed the cause as a rare autoimmune disorder that caused swelling in her brain and spinal cord. They told her family that she would be a vegetable for the rest of her life, and that there was a good possibility she wouldn't live long.

Despite the devastating news, Victoria's family believed that God was still in control and that He could restore her health. Her parents and brothers continued to talk to her as though she were still there and kept telling her that they loved her. Month after month went by, with no sign of anything changing. Two years later, this young lady woke up on the inside. She still couldn't move or open her eyes, and it didn't look as though anything had changed. But now she was aware of everything that was going on around her. Victoria was trapped inside her own body, unable to tell people that she was awake again. She could hear the doctors telling her parents that she was gone and there was no chance of recovery. She could hear her mother telling her that she loved her and she was going to make it. Every Sunday her mother would turn on the television to our services. Victoria would hear us talking about how God is our healer, how what was meant for harm He'll use for our advantage, how trouble is just transportation.

All through the day, lying in her bed paralyzed, trapped in her motionless body, instead of feeling sorry for herself, Victoria would say in her mind, *I'm a victor and not a victim*. Thoughts would tell her, *You're trapped. You'll never get out*. She would answer back, *No, my time is coming. This is not how my story ends*. She prayed that she could give her family a sign that she was in there. Three years after her body shut down, she was able to open her eyes, but she still had no other movement. Her mom asked her a question and said, "If you can understand, blink once for yes." She blinked once, and they knew she was still there. That was the start of a long journey back. She learned how to speak again, move again, and eat again. In September 2010, four years after she had become sick, she was able to go back to school. Everything woke up except her legs. She was paralyzed from the waist down. She was happy to be in a wheelchair, grateful to be out, but she wasn't satisfied. She knew that what God had started, He was going to finish. She was told that she would never be able to walk, but through prayer, extraordinarily hard work, and thousands of hours of training, in November 2015 she took a small step. In March 2016 she defied the odds, let go of her crutches, and took her first steps without assistance. Now she no longer needs the wheelchair or crutches, and she walks as though nothing were ever wrong.

After a ten-year journey, this beautiful twenty-one-year-old lady became one of the youngest on-air personalities for ESPN. She's also an actress, a model, and a motivational speaker. Friend, trouble is transportation. Victoria told me, "I wouldn't choose what happened to me, but

> *The God who brought her out is the God who's going to bring you out.*

I wouldn't change it." It was meant for harm, but God turned it around and used it for good. You may feel as though you're trapped in your circumstances, trapped in an addiction, trapped in depression, trapped in mediocrity. It doesn't feel as though anybody can hear you. You don't think you'll ever get out. But as was true for Victoria, that's not how your story ends. The God who brought her out is the God who's going to bring you out. I believe some dreams are waking up, hope is waking up, healing is waking up, abundance is waking up. That trouble is not going to stop you. It's going to push you into a level of your destiny that you would never have experienced without it. As with Victoria, you wouldn't choose what you've been through, but when you see how God pays you back, when you see the new doors that open, when you see how He turns it to your advantage, you'll say, "I wouldn't change it."

Shake off the self-pity, shake off the discouragement. You're anointed for that trouble. You may not understand what's happening. It may feel as though you're going in the wrong direction, but God is in control. That trouble is not going to get the best of you. It may look like a setback, but really it's a setup for God to do something greater. If you'll trust God in the trouble, that trouble is going to become transportation. God is going to open new doors, turn impossible situations around, and take you to the fullness of your destiny.

CHAPTER TEN

Dropped but Not Forgotten

We all go through situations in which life is not fair. I met a man a while ago who had just been laid off after twenty-five years with his company. He had been a faithful employee, giving it his best, loyal as could be. He felt betrayed, alone, and forgotten, as though he'd been dropped. He's not alone in feeling that way. I have a friend whose father was killed in an accident when he was two years old, and all through school he thought, *Why does everybody else have a dad, but I don't?* There was an emptiness on the inside. He felt dropped as a little boy.

Sometimes other people's poor choices have a negative effect on us. Maybe you were raised in an unhealthy environment, and now you're dealing with the same addictions, same depression, and same anger that surrounded you every day when you were a child. Those things keep getting passed down from generation to generation. Some people were taken advantage of and mistreated; now they deal with shame and guilt, feeling as though they don't measure up. It wasn't their fault. Somebody dropped them. I've learned you can't live very long without being dropped—dropped by an illness, dropped by a divorce, dropped by a friend who turns on you. It's easy to get stuck in a dark place, thinking, *This is never going to change. It's my lot in life.*

You may have been dropped, but the good news is that the God we serve knows how to pick you back up. David said, "God lifted me out of a horrible pit, and set my feet upon a rock." David was dropped by people coming against him, by rejection, by disappointments, and by his own failures, but God said, in effect, "Don't worry, David, that drop is not the end." In the same way, that bad break, that failure, those people who did you wrong, that sickness, that addiction, that chronic pain is not the end of your story.

If you have been dropped, you need to get ready. God's about to lift you. He's about to set you in a higher place. He's going to take you where you could not go on your own—to a new level, to new opportunities, to new friendships, to new health, to new joy, to new fulfillment. You're not going to come out the same. The Scripture talks about how God will pay you back double for the unfair things that happened. When you have a bad break and you get dropped, don't get discouraged or bitter. Get ready for double. Get ready for increase. Get ready for favor. Get ready for new levels.

God has not forgotten about you. He has seen every lonely night, every wrong that's been done, and every person who's ever harmed you. He's a God of justice. When the Israelites were being mistreated in slavery, taken advantage of by the Egyptians, He told them, "I'm coming down to make your wrongs right. I'm coming down to pick you back up. I'm coming down to bring justice, to deal with the people who have done you wrong." Did you notice what causes God to get off the throne, what causes the Creator of the universe to stop what He's doing and take action? When He sees you being mistreated, when He sees that injustice, He doesn't sit back and say, "Too bad." He says, "That's My son, that's My daughter, My most prized possession. They've been dropped, and now I have to get down there to do something about it." When God goes to work, all the forces of darkness cannot stop Him. He'll make your wrongs right, He'll pay you back for the trouble, and He'll get you to where you're supposed to be.

The fact is, we all get dropped in life. It's easy

It's easy to feel alone and forgotten, as though you don't matter. But don't believe those lies.

to feel alone and forgotten, as though you don't matter. But don't believe those lies. God said in the book of Isaiah, "I will not forget you. See, I have you carved in the palms of My hands." Every time God opens His hands, He sees your name. He's reminded of you. You may have had some bad breaks, some closed doors, some people who didn't do you right, but God hasn't forgotten about your dreams, He hasn't forgotten about the promises He's given you. He hasn't forgotten about that baby you've been longing to have, that spouse you've been praying for, that healing, that wholeness, that freedom you need. Stay in faith. Life happens to all of us, and you may get dropped, but remember that it's only temporary. God sees it. He's not only going to lift you back up, but He's going to take you to a higher place of blessing. You're going to come out better than you were before.

Nothing Goes Unnoticed

This is what happened to a young man in the Scripture named Mephibosheth. He was the grandson of King Saul and the son of Jonathan. Born into royalty, he was destined to one day take the throne. His future was bright. As a child he was cared for by loving nurses and people who treated him with kindness, doing their best to meet his every need. They knew they were dealing with the future king. But when he was five years old, his father, Jonathan, and grandfather King Saul were both killed in a battle. A messenger came to Mephibosheth's house telling the bad news and that the enemy was on its way to wipe out all of King Saul's family. A nurse picked up little Mephibosheth and in a panic took off running as fast as she could to try to save the boy's life. She had good intentions, she was trying to help him, but in her haste as they fled, she dropped Mephibosheth. Both of his legs were broken, and he became crippled and could no longer walk.

Mephibosheth didn't do anything wrong. It wasn't his fault. Yet he had to pay the price for somebody else's mistake for the rest of his life. It didn't seem fair. Sometimes well-meaning people can drop us. They don't mean to hurt us, but perhaps they made a mistake and said or did something they shouldn't have. They were working

> *Sometimes well-meaning people can drop us. They don't mean to hurt us, but perhaps they made a mistake and said or did something they shouldn't have.*

hard, struggling to make ends meet, and they weren't there when we needed them. Or they had bad habits, addictions that were passed down to them, which they've now passed down to us. They weren't bad people, their hearts were for us, but like this nurse they dropped us. Now we're crippled with low self-esteem, with addictions, with negativity, with depression. It's keeping us from our destiny.

Mephibosheth was the grandson of the king, had royalty in his blood, and was destined for the palace. But he ended up living in a place called Lo Debar, which was one of the poorest, most run-down cities of that day, a dark place. Year after year went by, and I'm sure he thought, *Everybody has forgotten about me. I used to be somebody important and respected. I used to have big dreams and was excited about life, but look at me now. I'm crippled and living in the slums. I don't have any friends, nobody cares about me, and none of this was even my fault. Somebody dropped me.* He felt alone and forgotten, as though it would never change.

But nothing goes unnoticed with our God. God saw that his father had been killed and taken away from him at an early age. God saw the well-meaning nurse drop him. God saw his once-normal legs, with which he could run, jump, and play, become crippled, resulting in his having to be carried around. God saw the poverty and lack he was living in. God didn't just sit back and say, "Boy, Mephibosheth, you sure had some bad breaks. You need to find a more sure-footed nurse next time. She really messed up your life." Rather, God said, "Mephibosheth, I haven't forgotten about you. I have you carved in the palms of My hands. You're always on My mind. Yes, you got dropped. Yes, life hasn't treated you fairly, but that bad break is not the end. I'm a God of justice. I'm going to pay you back for what's happened."

Many years later, King David had won great victories, established himself on the throne of Israel, was living in the palace, and was highly respected by the people. David didn't need anything; he had it all. But one day he had a desire to show kindness to Saul's family. Think about how unusual this was. Saul was the one who had tried to kill David. Saul was the one who had chased him through the wilderness and made his life miserable. Yet David said in 2 Samuel 9, "Is there anyone left from the house of Saul, that I might show kindness to?" Why would David want to be good to the family of one of his enemies? That didn't make sense. But God is a God of justice. He controls the whole universe. That was God whispering in David's ear, putting a desire in him to be good to someone who had been dropped—namely, Mephibosheth.

God knows how to make things happen that

You may have been dropped, but don't be discouraged. Justice is coming, restoration is coming, promotion is coming, favor is coming, and new beginnings are coming.

you could never make happen. You may say, "Joel, I'm stuck in a dark place. I've had these bad breaks, and I'm never going to get out of this mess, never going to accomplish my dreams, and never going to be fulfilled." No, your time is coming. God is going to whisper in someone's ear to be good to you. You don't deserve it, you won't earn it, and you couldn't make it happen on your own, but somebody will give you a good break, somebody will offer you the job, somebody will give you the contract, somebody will step up and solve the problem. You may have been dropped, but don't be discouraged. Justice is coming, restoration is coming, promotion is coming, favor is coming, and new beginnings are coming.

The King Is Summoning You

When David asked if any of Saul's relatives were still alive, his assistant said, "We've searched and searched, and there's only one grandson left, the son of Jonathan. His name is Mephibosheth. But the problem is, he's crippled. He can't walk. He's never going to amount to much. No use wasting your time with him." They tried to talk David out of it, but he said, "No. Go get him and bring him to my palace."

Mephibosheth had been hiding, living in exile, hoping that nobody would know he was related to King Saul. After all, Saul had not treated David right. Imagine what people thought when the officials from the palace, wearing their royal uniforms, showed up in Lo Debar and started going through the slums looking for this crippled man. The whole town was stirring, buzzing with excitement. Word finally reached Mephibosheth: "Someone is here from the palace." He asked, "What are they doing here of all places?" They answered back, "They're looking for you." Mephibosheth's heart skipped a beat. He thought, *Oh man, my luck has run out. They found me. Now they're going to get rid of me.* The officials said, "Come with us right now. The king is summoning you."

The problem was that Mephibosheth couldn't walk. They had to carry him to the palace. They spent hours and hours traveling and finally made it to the palace. When they told David that he'd arrived, David went out to meet him. I'm sure that David was expecting to see a tall, strong, good-looking man who stood head and shoulders above the rest of the people, like his grandfather King Saul. Saul had looked like a king, had a presence that commanded respect, and walked as royalty. Now here comes his grandson. Surely there would be some resemblance. But when David saw the frail Mephibosheth, with his shriveled-up legs, I can imagine him asking his assistant, "Are you sure this is Saul's grandson? Are you sure he's royalty? Is he really Jonathan's son?" If this story took place today, they would have answered, "Yes, we're positive. We went to ancestry.com. We did DNA testing." David was very puzzled and asked, "Mephibosheth?" His question clearly implied, "What happened to you?" Mephibosheth wouldn't look David in the eyes, having fallen on his face on the ground. He was too ashamed, too insecure, too afraid. He said, "King David, when I was five years old and my father and grandfather were killed, I was dropped, and my life has never been the same."

That could have been the end of the story. David could have said, "Too bad. You should have seen how your grandfather treated me. I don't feel sorry for you. You're getting what your family deserved." Mephibosheth was so afraid that he was shaking, thinking it was the end, but

"From now on you're not going to live in Lo Debar. You're going to live here in the palace with me."

David said, "Mephibosheth, don't fear. I'm not going to harm you. I'm going to show you kindness for Jonathan your father's sake. From now on you're not going to live in Lo Debar. You're going to live here in the palace with me. I'm going to give you all the land that belonged to your grandfather King Saul. You don't have to go out and work the land. I'm going to give you a full staff that will farm the land for you, and you will keep all the profits. They'll do the work, and you reap the benefits. And last thing, you will always sit at my table and have dinner with me—not over with the staff, not with my assistants or with the military leaders. You have a permanent seat at the king's table."

There's a Seat for You at the King's Table

Maybe you feel as though you've been dropped in a way similar to Mephibosheth. Perhaps you had a bad break, lost a loved one, or weren't treated right. It would be easy to get bitter, settle there, and not expect anything good. You need to get ready, for your time is coming. The King is about to summon you to the palace. God is going to pay you back, and not just what should have been yours. He's going to give you what belonged to your forefathers. It's going to be far and beyond favor. You're not going to have to work for it. It will be the goodness of God, paying you back and bringing justice. You may not see how it can happen, but God is speaking to the right people about you. He's softening the right hearts. He's going to pay you back for that unfair childhood, pay you back for those people who did you wrong, pay you back for that loved one you lost, pay you back for that baby you couldn't have. You may have been dropped, but you need to get ready, for there's a seat at the King's table waiting for you. God's already prepared it, and it has your name on it. It's a seat of favor, a seat of restoration, a seat of healing, a seat of increase.

You have royal blood in your veins. The Most High God breathed His life into you. He's crowned you with favor and destined you to live in the palace. That is a place of blessing, a place of wholeness, a place of victory. So don't settle in Lo Debar, don't get comfortable just surviving, enduring, barely making it in that dark place. "Well, Joel, I've had some bad breaks. Life hasn't turned out fair." Maybe not, but that doesn't change who you are. You're still royalty. You still have the crown of favor. You still have the

> *There is going to be a lifting out of the pit. Things will happen for you that you couldn't make happen.*

DNA of Almighty God. It's payback time. There's a seat at the King's table with your name on it. People may have pushed you down, but God's going to push you up. Circumstances may have dropped you, but God is the glory and the lifter of your head. Just as with the Israelite slaves in Egypt, He's coming down to make things right. There is going to be a lifting out of the pit. Things will happen for you that you couldn't make happen. The favor of God will open new doors, causing people to be good to you, paying you back for the unfair situations.

What's interesting is that Mephibosheth was never healed. For the rest of his life he remained a cripple. It may seem as though this isn't a good ending. But I've learned that if God doesn't remove the difficulty, if He doesn't totally turn it around, He will make it up to you. You may have lost a loved one; you can't bring that person back, but God can make the rest of your life so rewarding, so fulfilling, that it takes away the pain. Perhaps a relationship didn't work out—a person walked out of your life and broke your heart. God can bring somebody new into your life who's so loving, so fun, so kind, so appealing to you, that you won't even miss the person who left you. God knows how to pay you back. Mephibosheth was never able to walk again, but sitting at the king's table each night, having people to take care of him, to farm his land and bring him the profit—for those reasons I don't think he ever complained. All he could say was, "Thank You, Lord, for Your goodness. Thank You for saving me. Thank You for rescuing me. Thank You for Your mercy." When God overwhelms you with His goodness, when He brings you out with double, you don't think about what you've lost, who hurt you, or what didn't work out. You're so amazed that God remembered you, promoted you, brought the right people when you didn't think you could go on and had them carry you to the palace—all you can do is thank Him for what He's done.

My sister Lisa and her husband, Kevin, tried for many years to have a baby with no success. She went through all the fertility treatments, had a couple of surgeries, but still no baby. Finally the doctors told them that she would never be able to have a child. Many people have received that same report, but against all the odds, they've had a baby anyway. They've seen God make a way where there was no way. But for Lisa and Kevin, it didn't happen. Lisa felt as though she had been dropped. But God is a God of justice. As was true for Mephibosheth, if you don't get healed, if it doesn't turn out your way, God will make it up to you. One day Lisa received a phone call from a friend in another state who runs a home for teenage girls. She said, "We have a young lady who's about to have twins, and something told me to call and see if you and Kevin would be interested in adopting them." When they heard that, something leaped in their spirits. They knew right then and there that those girls were for them. A couple of years later, they also adopted a baby boy. Now they have three amazing teenagers, as happy as can be. Lisa said, "Here's how good God is. I have three children, and I never had to get pregnant once."

God knows how to make it up to you. Don't get bitter or wallow around in self-pity. God hasn't forgotten about you. When He pays you back, it will be bigger, better, and more rewarding than you can imagine. You won't complain about the disappointment. Rather you'll be saying, "Look what the Lord has done. He's amazed me with His goodness."

You Have a Ticket Out of Lo Debar

Mephibosheth was summoned to the palace, but he couldn't get there on his own—he was carried to the palace. Each night at dinnertime, he couldn't get to his seat by himself—he was carried to the table. When he went to sleep at night, he was carried to his bed. You may think, *I can't accomplish my dreams.*

I'm crippled. I'm broken. I have these addictions. I'm dealing with this depression, this sickness. But when you can't do it on your own, God will always have somebody there to carry you. You're not alone, and you're not forgotten. God has you in the palms of His hands. He's not looking down on you because you're crippled, so to speak. You're struggling in some areas. He saw the times you've been dropped. You didn't go down by yourself, and you're not going to come up by yourself. God has people already lined up to carry you, to encourage you, to help you do what you could not do on your own.

When Jesus was carrying the cross and about to be crucified, He was so exhausted, so weak, that He collapsed under the weight of the cross. He couldn't carry it any farther. There was a man named Simon who just happened to be right there. He picked up the cross and carried it the rest of the way. You don't have to be strong all the time. Even Jesus fell down under the weight of the cross.

> *The good news is that there will always be somebody there to help you, to carry you, to get you to where you need to be.*

The good news is that there will always be somebody there to help you, to carry you, to get you to where you need to be. In the Garden of Gethsemane on the previous night, Jesus had been in so much distress that His sweat became like great drops of blood. On the cross Jesus felt alone, forgotten, and abandoned. At one point He cried out, "My God, My God, why have You forsaken Me?" He had been mistreated, falsely accused, and rejected. He was saying, "God, I've been dropped. I feel forgotten, alone, up here by Myself." It looked as though that were the end and the darkness had won, but three days later, Jesus was sitting at the King's table, the victor, not the victim. The enemy never has the final say. God controls the universe. He's a God of justice.

When you don't have the strength to move forward on your own, God has angels to carry you. He has the right people lined up to help you. He's not going to let you stay in Lo Debar. He's going to keep working, restoring, promoting, and increasing you until He gets you to your seat at the King's table. Dinner is not complete without you there. You may have been dropped, you may have had bad breaks, you may feel broken and crippled, but that's okay. Today you're being summoned by the King. We need your presence. We need your gifts. We need your smile, your laughter, your love, and your kindness—not half-hearted or pushed down.

This is a new day. Isaiah said, "God will give you joy instead of mourning, a crown of beauty instead of ashes, a garment of praise instead of a spirit of heaviness." Maybe you don't have enough joy, there's not enough laughter, and you're letting your circumstances and pressures weigh you down. But I believe that God is breathing new life into your spirit. The sadness is leaving and gladness is coming. Heaviness is going and joy is on the way. Your life is going to be filled with laughter and happiness. The Scripture says you will have joy unspeakable and full of glory.

You Are Not Forgotten

Many years ago, there was a young man in South Korea who was dying from tuberculosis. One of his lungs had already collapsed. As he lay on his bed at home waiting to die, he was in so much pain that he began to call out to his gods one by one. He cried out to one god, "Please, come help me!" No answer. He called out to another god, but still no answer. Finally, in desperation, he said in the dark emptiness of his room, "If there's any god out there anywhere, I don't ask you to heal me. I just ask you to show me how to die." He felt alone and forgotten. He had been dropped through no fault of his own, by a life-threatening disease.

You might not think that God would have anything to do with this young man. After all, he wasn't a believer. But the Scripture says, "Call on God, and He will answer you." It doesn't say call if you go to church, or call

> *He has a seat for you at the King's table.*

if you can quote the Scripture, or call if you're good enough. No, it says that anyone is welcome to call. God breathed His life into you. He has a seat for you at the King's table. A few hours later, a young college student was walking through the neighborhood and felt what she described as an unexplainable love drawing her to that man's house. She knocked on the door, and his mother answered. The college student said, "I know you don't know me, but I just wanted to know if there's anything I can pray with you about." The mother began to weep and told how her son was on his deathbed. The young lady went in and prayed for him. He gave his life to Christ. Long story short: God healed him, and today, many years later, Dr. David Yonggi Cho is the founding pastor of the largest church in the world.

Friend, God hasn't forgotten about you. He's a God of justice. You may be dealing with a sickness, a loss, or a bad break. You may feel as though life has dropped you, but you need to get ready. God is about to pick you back up, and He is not just going to bring you out the same—He's going to set you on high and bring you out better. It's payback time. God is about to make some things up to you. He's lining up the right people to come find you with blessings, with favor. I believe that as Mephibosheth did, you're coming into the palace—a place of healing, a place of restoration, abundance, opportunity, and new levels. You're going to take your seat at the King's table and see the goodness of God in amazing ways.

CHAPTER ELEVEN

Balanced Books

In accounting, the term *balancing the books* means making up for a loss. If an account is low, if there's a deficit, when you balance the books, you add revenue to even it out. To know how much the account is behind, you have to first take all the losses, all the deficits, and total them up. Then you know how much you need to add to balance it. One definition of *balancing the books* is "to equalize, to experience no loss." When the books are balanced, nobody can tell there's ever been a loss. There is no deficit.

In the same way, God has promised that He will balance the books of our lives. We all go through things that put us at a deficit—situations that are unfair, a rough childhood, a friend who walks out on us, the loss of a loved one. If nothing changed, we would be out of balance. We would go through life with more loss, thinking, *Too bad for me. I got the short end of the stick.* A young lady told me that she's had six miscarriages and is not able to carry a baby to term. With big tears running down her cheeks, she said, "I don't understand it. I want to have a baby so bad." Life is not always fair, but God is fair. He will add up all the losses, the disappointments, the heartaches, and the tears, and He will pay you back.

In Hebrews 10, the writer notes that the people had endured a severe time of suffering and persecution. Some of them have lost their homes and some have been imprisoned. He encourages them by saying that the time will come when they will be richly rewarded. He says, in essence, "God is a just God. He will repay the compensation owed us. He will settle the cases of His people." God knows what you're owed. You're not going to live in a deficit. You may go through seasons when you're out of balance—you have a disappointment, a loss, something that doesn't make sense—but don't worry about it. Your time is coming. God is going to settle your case. He's seen every tear you've shed, every person who did you wrong, every injustice, every dark place. Nobody

You're not going to end up in the red—lonely, disappointed, at a disadvantage. That's all temporary.

else may know a thing about it, but God knows. He's not going to leave you out of balance. You're not going to end up in the red—lonely, disappointed, at a disadvantage. That's all temporary. The Creator of the universe is adding up all the deficits. You may have been through things you don't understand, and you could easily be discouraged and feel sorry for yourself. Instead, get your passion back. God is saying, "I'm about to balance your books." Compensation is coming, promotion is coming, vindication is coming, healing is coming, blessing is coming.

Justice Is Coming

I can look back on my life and see times when God balanced my books. When I was growing up, we had church in a small run-down building that had been a feed store. It had spiderwebs and holes in the floor, and you could sweep the feed through the cracks. We cleaned it up, and for thirteen years we had services there. Over time that area of northeast Houston went downhill and wasn't kept up very well. My family lived thirty minutes away from the church. Most of my schoolmates went to a nearby neighborhood church. It was a beautiful, prestigious brick church, with stained glass

windows and a huge pipe organ. Some people considered us second class, thinking, *They can't afford
a nice place to meet. They're in that old run-down
building.* I would occasionally hear them making
fun of us, joking about our building. They were
good people, but they dismissed us, saw us as less
than. In their book we were not up to par.

Fast-forward thirty years and we're no longer
in a run-down wooden building, because God has
given us the Compaq Center—the premier facility
in our city, in the most prestigious part of town.
That was God balancing the books. That was God
bringing justice. When I was growing up, it never
bothered me when I heard people make fun of our
church. I didn't pay any attention to it. But God
pays attention. He's keeping track of who's trying
to push you down, to discredit you, to make you
look small. He knows who's talking behind your
back. He's adding up all the deficits, and at the
right time He's going to balance your books.

God is going to pay you back not just for wrongs
done to you, but also for what your parents put up
with, for injustices done to those who went before
you. My father never saw the level of influence
that God has blessed me with. I recognize that
I'm reaping what he sowed. This is God balancing
the books in our family. There are people in your
family line who did the right thing but for whom

the wrong thing happened. They served, gave, and honored God, but they didn't see total justice. Get ready, because God is going to bless you, as He did me, to make up for what should have been theirs. God is not going to leave your family unbalanced. There will be times when you come into blessings that you didn't deserve, good breaks that you didn't work for, open doors that never should have opened. It wasn't anything that you did; that was God paying your family back what it was owed.

You're Coming Out, and You Won't Be Empty-Handed

This is what happened with the Israelites. For ten generations they had been in slavery in Egypt. They were mistreated, taken advantage of, forced to work long hours, given quotas that were impossible to meet. After 430 years, God delivered them from slavery. Just the fact that they were finally free and able to leave was a great miracle. But they didn't leave as broke, empty-handed slaves, with their heads hanging down in shame. They had worked all that time without being paid. They were owed a whole lot. God said, "All right, it's time to balance the books." On their way out, God caused them to have favor with their captors—the same

Suddenly their captors had a change of heart and gave them their gold, their silver, their jewels, and their clothing. The Israelites left the dark place of slavery behind, pushing wheelbarrows full of treasures.

people who had mistreated them, the same ones who had looked down on them and made their lives miserable. Suddenly their captors had a change of heart and gave them their gold, their silver, their jewels, and their clothing. The Israelites left the dark place of slavery behind, pushing wheelbarrows full of treasures. That was God balancing the books, paying them back for those 430 years.

God sees every deficit, every wrong done to you and your family. He knows what you're owed. As with the Israelites, there will be a time when He says, "Enough is enough. It's time to balance the books." He's promised that He's going to compensate you. Quit worrying about who did you wrong, what you didn't get, who put you at a disadvantage, and who's not giving you the credit. God knows what happened, and He's saying, "It's payback time. You're coming out, and you won't be empty-handed, looked down upon, or seen as second class. You're coming out vindicated, promoted, respected, with abundance." You'll receive favor that you don't deserve, with blessings chasing you down. That's the God of justice compensating you with what you're owed.

A young man told me about how he was raised in a negative environment. His father hadn't ever been in his life, and his mother was never around, having plenty of issues of her own. He didn't understand why he'd been dealt this hand in life, and why he was put at such a disadvantage. I told him what I'm telling you. Life may not be fair, but God is fair. He knows what you've been through, and He's going to make it up to you. But here's the key: you can't go around with a chip on your shoulder, thinking about what your mama and daddy didn't give you. God knows what they didn't give you. If you'll stay in faith, God will balance your books. He'll pay you back. God is a God of justice. If you didn't get much in a certain area, He'll give you more in another area to make up for it.

You may feel as though you were shortchanged as well—you didn't have a good childhood, or you're dealing with a health issue, or your boss hasn't treated you fairly. The good news is, God sees what you're owed. He's keeping the records. He may not be able to give you another childhood or bring

Balancing the books means you're not living in a place of loss or deficit, always thinking about what you're lacking and how you're at a disadvantage.

back a loved one whom you lost, but He can make the rest of your life so rewarding, so fulfilling, that you don't think about what didn't work out. Balancing the books means you're not living in a place of loss or deficit, always thinking about what you're lacking and how you're at a disadvantage.

When my father went to be with the Lord in 1999, I lost one of my best friends. I'd worked with him for seventeen years, and we'd traveled the world together. But even though I miss my father today, even though I'd love for him to be here, God has blessed me in so many other areas that I'm not living from a place of deficit. For the first year or so, I was unbalanced—that loss was heavy. But God began to bring new gifts out of me, opened up new doors, and caused things to fall into place. What was happening? He was balancing my books.

Payback Is Coming

Maybe somebody walked out of a relationship with you and broke your heart. Don't give up on life, and don't go around bitter. God saw the hurt, and He feels your pain. It's not the end. You may be unbalanced right now, the discouragement may be heavy, but the good news is, God is going to balance your books. Payback is coming. Somebody better than you imagined is coming your way. Maybe a dream didn't work out, or you didn't get the scholarship, or you're raising a special needs child and never thought that would happen. Perhaps you received a medical report that wasn't good, and now you have to take another round of treatment. In those tough times, those dark times when life doesn't seem fair, you have to keep reminding yourself that God is a God of justice. He knows exactly what's going on. You're not going to live in a place of deficit. All through the day, just say, "Father, I want to thank You that You're balancing my books. Lord, I believe payback is coming, restoration is coming, healing is coming." That attitude of faith is what allows God to pay you back for what you're owed. You're not sitting around in self-pity, blaming others and living discouraged. The hand you've been dealt may not be fair, but it's not a surprise to God. He already has a way to settle your case. Every time you're tempted to worry, just turn it around and thank Him that payback is on the way, thank Him that you're coming into a place of no loss.

I talked to a lady who had been married for fourteen years and has beautiful children. Life was good. But one day out of the blue her husband told her that he was leaving her for another woman. She was totally blindsided. She had been a stay-at-home mom and hadn't been in the workforce for over ten years. She didn't know what she was going to do or how she could provide for her children. A few weeks later, while she was still numb, trying to take it all in, a former friend from high school, whom she hadn't talked to in twenty years, contacted her. This woman said, "I'm starting a new business, and out of nowhere your name came to mind. I'm wondering if you would be interested in being my business partner." Her friend had been very successful in other businesses. The lady told how she was going through a divorce and didn't have any funds to invest in a business. Her friend said, "I don't need any money. I have all the funds necessary. I just want you to work with me." Their business took off, and today this lady is incredibly blessed. She has plenty to take care of her family.

God knows how to balance your books. He didn't promise that unfair things wouldn't happen to you, but He did promise He would compensate you with what you're owed. You're not going to live in a deficit. He's going to settle your accounts. He's already lined up the right people to search you out. He can make things happen that you could never make happen. You may have gone through a disappointment, a bad break, and maybe somebody didn't treat you right. Get ready. Payback is coming. Vindication is on the way.

Nothing Goes Unnoticed

Back in chapter three, we considered a lady in the Old Testament named Leah. She and her sister, Rachel, were both married to Jacob. Rachel was far more beautiful, and Jacob didn't give Leah much time and attention. I'm sure that Leah felt as though she were not good enough, inferior, at a disadvantage. She hadn't gotten her sister's looks. The Scripture says, "When the Lord saw that Leah was unloved, He enabled her to have children, while Rachel was childless." Leah went on to have six sons and a daughter before Rachel was able to have a child. Having a son was a big deal back in those days. God was saying, "Leah, because your husband is not treating you right, because you didn't get beautiful looks like your sister, I'm going to balance your books and give you something that causes Jacob to notice you. I'm going to enable you to have children before your sister."

What am I saying? God gives special favor to people at a disadvantage. You may feel as though someone else got all the good breaks—the good childhood, the good looks, the winning personality. Don't worry. Your time is coming. God has some advantages for you that will cause you to stand out. You're not going to live always in the shadow of somebody more talented, more beautiful, or more successful. God is going to cause you to shine. You're going to excel, you're going to be known, you're going to leave your mark. What you think you didn't get in looks, in personality, in education, or in your upbringing, God is going to make it up to you. He's going to balance your books.

As with Leah, when people don't treat you right, when they look down on you, dismiss you, and try to make you feel small, that doesn't go unnoticed. God sees every injustice, every wrong, every tear, every bad break. The Scripture says that a sparrow doesn't fall to the ground without God's knowing it. How much more does God see everything that happens to you? When somebody does you wrong, God takes it personally. You're His child. He doesn't sit back and say, "Too bad. They shouldn't treat them that way." He goes to work much as we do as parents if somebody mistreats our children. We may even go a little overboard to make things right.

Once when our daughter, Alexandra, was four years old, I bought her an ice cream cone. We walked outside the store and stopped to talk with some friends. There were some other kids on the sidewalk, running around and eating their ice cream. I noticed one little boy was playing rough with everybody. I thought, *You better watch out, because that's my little girl over there.* Even though I was involved in a conversation, about half of my attention was watching this other scene. As the kids were running around, at one point the little boy bumped into Alexandra, and she dropped her ice cream cone. He laughed and thought it was funny, then he began to make fun of her because she didn't have any ice cream. Alexandra came straight over to me, knowing that I would make things right. We went back into the store. Normally I would get her one scoop of ice cream, but this time I said, "We're going to get three scoops so you'll have more than anyone else." She took her three-scoop cone, found that little boy, and started waving it in front of him as though saying, "Look what you did. You caused me to get three times what I had before!" That little boy meant it for harm, but I meant it for good. That's the way God is. Somebody may have done you wrong, but stay in peace. God is going to pay you back. He knows what you're owed. God never brings you out the same. He always makes the enemy pay. He'll bring you out better.

Your Enemies Will End Up
Shaking Your Hand

The prophet Isaiah said, "Because you got a double dose of trouble, your inheritance in the land will

> *"Because you got a double dose of trouble, your inheritance in the land will be double, and your joy will go on forever."*

be double, and your joy will go on forever." Don't complain about the trouble; that difficulty set you up for double. That bad break and disappointment may look like a setback, but really it was a setup for God to show out in a new way. He's about to balance some books. When there are people in your life who have been against you, some of them for years, and have tried to hold you down, make you look bad, discredit you—things are about to change. God is going to cause them to see you in a new light. He's going to cause them to recognize His blessing on your life to a point where they treat you with the respect and honor you deserve.

When the Israelites were stuck in the darkness of slavery, Moses told Pharaoh again and again to let God's people go, but Pharaoh wouldn't listen. He didn't respect Moses. He thought, *Who are you to tell me what to do? I'm the Pharaoh. I'm a world leader. I have the royal robe on. I live in the palace. You're a shepherd. You don't have any credentials. You're not successful, you live out in the desert, and you look as though you've been wearing the same clothes for forty years. You're nothing compared to me.* He dismissed Moses as second class. This happened over and over. Every time Moses went back to tell him another plague was coming, Pharaoh didn't pay any attention to him. He thought, *Here comes that crazy Moses trying to tell me what to do again.* What's interesting is that after the last plague, when Pharaoh finally decided to let the Hebrew people go, not only did the Egyptians give the Israelites their gold and silver, but Pharaoh said, "Moses, take all your flocks and herds, as you have said, and go, and ask your God to bless me also." Instead of making fun of Moses, instead of seeing him as not good enough, now Pharaoh recognized the hand of God on Moses. He saw the anointing and felt the power to where he asked Moses to bless him!

Part of God's balancing your books is that people who didn't respect you, who dismissed you, and who discredited you are going to have a change of heart and ask for your blessing. They're going to recognize the favor on your life. The Scripture says, "God can turn the heart of a king wherever He wishes." God knows how to change people. You don't have

As Moses did, you will see a day when the person who disrespected you the most, the Pharaoh who wouldn't give you the time of day and who wouldn't bother to even look at you, will ask for your blessing.

to play up to them, or try to convince them to like you, or let them control and manipulate you in order to try to win their favor. No, walk in your anointing. Run your own race, always honoring God with excellence and integrity. God will turn the hearts of those who are against you. It may not happen overnight. It may take years, but God will balance your books. As Moses did, you will see a day when the person who disrespected you the most, the Pharaoh who wouldn't give you the time of day and who wouldn't bother to even look at you, will ask for your blessing. Proverbs says, "When a man's ways please the Lord, He makes even his enemies to be at peace with him." Don't get upset when people try to belittle you, push you down, or act disrespectful. Just keep honoring God, and one day they'll ask for your blessing. One paraphrase says, "Your enemies will end up shaking your hand."

One Sunday I met a man after the service who was a pastor in another state. He told me he had been our biggest critic and used to tell his congregation not to watch our services on television.

He was very outspoken and wrote articles against us. But a couple of years ago he went through a major health crisis and had to give up his church. He didn't know if he was going to live through it. One night while he was flipping through the channels, he came across our program, and he said that for the first time he really watched it closely. He said, "Joel, I haven't turned you off since. Now I'm your biggest supporter. I tell everybody about you. You helped me get through the most difficult time in my life." He gave me a big hug and said, "Will you pray for me?" That's what the Scripture says. When you honor God, one day your enemies will end up shaking your hand. God knows how to make the people who are against you need what you have. Instead of knocking you, they'll support you.

Balancing the Books Requires Extending Your Blessing

In the Scripture, a man named Saul was the biggest enemy of the early church. He went around having believers arrested and put in jail. Nobody was more opposed to the followers of Christ than he. When the high priest and Sanhedrin stoned Stephen to death for preaching about Jesus, Saul was standing right there giving his approval. One

day Saul was headed toward Damascus with letters
in hand authorizing him to arrest believers. But
in the middle of the journey, a bright light from
heaven flashed around him, he fell to the ground,
and when he opened his eyes he could see nothing.
He was blind. The men traveling with him led
him by the hand to Damascus. For three days he
was so distraught he went without food and water.

Meanwhile, in Damascus, a believer named Ananias saw a vision in which the Lord told him to go
to the house where Saul was staying and place his
hands on him to restore his sight. Ananias went and
prayed for him, and Saul could see again. Notice
what God did. Saul is sitting there blind, and now
the one person who has the answer to his prayer is
one of the Christian disciples he came to arrest. Saul
had been Ananias's biggest critic and would have
gladly had him imprisoned and even put to death,
but now he needed what Ananias had. Instead of
wanting to persecute Ananias, I'm sure that Saul
had been praying, "Lord Jesus, please send one of
Your believers to come and pray for me. I am willing to follow You, but I don't know what to do."

You may have people like Saul in your life who
have been against you for years. They may not be
that menacing or vocal, but they're condescend-
ing toward you and treat you as though you're
less than. Don't worry. Payback is coming. God is

your vindicator. Keep taking the high road, keep doing the right thing, and one day they'll need what you have. They'll come to you in humility, asking for your help, your blessing, your favor.

When the Lord told Ananias in the vision to go and pray for Saul, he could have responded, "God, I've heard all about this guy and all the harm he's done to Your people in Jerusalem. Do You realize who he is? This is a setup. He's going

Will you be good to that Saul in your life when he needs what you have?

to arrest me." God said, "No, it's not what you think. Things have changed. I'm going to use Saul in a great way." Ananias went and prayed for his biggest enemy. He did good to somebody who had spent years doing bad to his fellow believers. This is a test we all have to pass. Will you be good to that Saul in your life when he needs what you have? Will you show him favor even though he hasn't treated you right, even though he's tried to make you look bad? If you want God to balance your books, you have to be the bigger person and bless those who have cursed you. In their time of need, don't withhold your help. Don't say, "Too bad for you, Saul. I'm glad you're blind. You deserve it. Now maybe you'll leave us alone." No, do good to those who persecute you. Ananias walked into the house and said, "Brother Saul." He called his main enemy a brother and treated him as his friend. After he prayed, Saul could once again see. Saul went on to become the apostle Paul, who wrote about half the books of the New Testament.

Your Time Is Coming

When people come against us and say things that are not true, it's easy to get frustrated and try to straighten them out and prove to them who we are. But don't waste your emotional energy on the Sauls in your life. Wait for God to do it His way. He sees every injustice, every negative word, and He's adding up all the deficits, all the wrongs. At the right time, He'll make things happen that you could never make happen. He'll cause them to need what you have.

Friend, your time is coming. You're not going to live in a deficit. You may have had some bad breaks, gone through things you don't understand. Take heart. The God of justice is saying, "It's pay-back time." I believe and declare God is going to balance your books. He's going to turn the darkest of situations around. He's going to open new doors of opportunity. Promotion is coming, vindication is coming. Because you honor Him, even your enemies are going to be at peace with you.

CHAPTER TWELVE

Faith for the Middle

It's easy to have faith at the start. When your new baby is born, or you marry that beautiful girl, or you start that new business, it's exciting. There's adrenaline flowing, and it feels great. It's also easy to have faith at the end. When you can see the finish line, you've fought the good fight, and now the dream is in sight. Having faith at the start and at the end is not a problem.

The challenge is having faith in the middle—when it's taking longer than you thought, when you don't have the funds, when the medical report isn't good. You were so excited about that cute little baby who could do no wrong. Now he's a teenager, and you're convinced that he's not your child. You're having his DNA tested next week. The mistake we make is that we get discouraged in the middle. We think, *God, I know You gave me this child, but he's making my life miserable. I know You brought my spouse into my life, but now there's conflict. I know You blessed me with this business, but now I don't have the funds I need.* In the middle is where most people lose the battle.

But God never promised that we would reach our destiny without opposition, without disappointments, without things we don't understand. The Scripture says, "Don't think it's strange when you face fiery trials." That means don't get upset because somebody did you wrong. Don't start worrying because the business slowed. Don't live in anxiety because your child has taken a wrong turn. God is still on the throne. Nothing that's happened to you has stopped His plan for your life. He's not up in heaven scratching His head and thinking, *Oh man, I didn't see that one coming. That bad break threw Me off.* What He promised you, He still has every intention of bringing to pass. I know you can have faith at the start—that's easy. I know you can have faith at the end. My question is, will you have faith in the middle? Will you have faith when it's not happening as you thought it would, when it feels as though you're going in the wrong direction and it's dark and difficult there, when every voice tells you to give up and says, "You must have heard God wrong." Don't believe those lies. It's all a part of the process.

When God puts a dream in your heart, He'll

show you the end. He'll give you the promise, but He won't show you the middle. If He told us all it would take for it to come to pass, we would talk ourselves out of it. In the Scripture an angel appeared to a teenager named Mary. He said, "Mary, you are highly favored of God. You will have a baby without knowing a man, and He will be the Messiah, the Savior of the world." God showed her the end. She was going to be the mother of Christ. She would have honor and be respected and admired for generations to come. I'm sure Mary was excited. She couldn't believe it. But I can hear Mary years later, saying, "God, You didn't tell me that having this baby was going to cause my fiancé to want to call off our engagement. You didn't tell me I would have this baby in a manger with smelly animals. You didn't tell me I would have to live on the run for two years, hiding my baby from King Herod. You didn't tell me my son would be mistreated, betrayed, and mocked. You didn't tell me I would have to watch Him be crucified and die a painful death."

What am I saying? God doesn't give us all the details. What you're going through may be difficult, you don't like it, it doesn't make sense. This is where your faith has to kick in. Are you going to give up and talk yourself out of it? Or are you going to do as

> *God doesn't give us all the details.*

Mary did and say, "God, I don't understand this. You didn't tell me this person was going to do me wrong or that I would be dealing with this sickness. You didn't tell me this business was going to slow down. But God, I know You're still on the throne, and it's not a surprise to You. I'm not going to live in discouragement, give up on my dreams, or quit believing. I'm going to have faith in the middle."

The Middle Can Be Messy

You remember what I said in chapter nine about Joseph. God gave him a dream that one day his father and mother and his eleven brothers would bow down before him. God showed him the end, and the promise was planted in his heart. But what God didn't show him was the middle. Years later, when Joseph was ruling over the nation of Egypt as one of the most powerful people of his day, the dream came to pass. I can hear Joseph saying, "God, You gave me this incredible promise, but You didn't tell me that my brothers would be jealous and throw me into a pit. You showed me that I would rule one day, but You didn't tell me that on the way I would be sold into slavery. You didn't tell me I would be falsely accused and put in prison." If Joseph were here today, he would tell you, "Don't get discouraged in the middle. Don't give up when life doesn't make sense." You know the promise is in your heart. You know God told you that you're going to be healthy again, you're going to see your family restored, you're going to meet the person of your dreams, but every circumstance says just the opposite. It feels as though you're moving backward. Keep believing, keep being your best. God has not brought you this far to leave you. He hasn't failed you in the past, and He's not going to fail you in the future. Don't get discouraged by the process.

The start is fun, and the end is exciting; but the truth is, the middle can be messy. In some way we're all in the middle; we're all on a journey. There are things that you're believing for—you know God has planted those seeds. Over time it's easy to give up and think, *There are too many obstacles. It's never going to happen.* God has you reading this to breathe new life into your dreams. What He's placed in your heart is already en route. The process has already been started. The right people, the healing, the breakthrough, the new business is on the way. Now do your part and have faith for the middle.

David could have said, "God, You promised me that I would be the king, but You didn't tell me that I would have to face a giant twice my size. You left that detail out. You didn't tell me that even though I was faithfully serving King Saul, he would try to kill me. You didn't tell me that my own son would turn on me and try to take the throne." When you study the heroes of faith, such as David and Joseph, one common denominator you'll find is that they had faith in the middle. When it looked impossible, when the promise seemed far off, they kept moving forward, knowing it was a part of the process. They weren't surprised by the trials or dark places. They weren't discouraged by opposition. Yes, they had their moments. They were as human as the rest of us. At times worry would come, fear would come, doubt would come, but they didn't allow it to stay. They stirred their faith back up and believed that the promise would happen.

> *When you study the heroes of faith, one common denominator you'll find is that they had faith in the middle.*

I remember where I was sitting in a restaurant when a friend of mine told me that the Compaq Center was going to be put on the real estate market by the city of Houston. As he was speaking, down deep inside I had this sense that that facility was meant for us. God showed me the end. I could see us having services there and touching the world. I look back now and realize that

God didn't show me that it was going to take two years to convince ten city council members to vote for us. He didn't show me that one of the largest companies in Texas would file a lawsuit to try to keep us from moving in. He didn't tell me that it was going to cost a hundred million dollars to renovate the center. Sometimes God leaves out certain details on purpose. If He had told me that I would be responsible for all that money, I would have said, "We're fine with our old facility." I would have settled for less than His best. There's a reason we don't have all the details. If we did, we wouldn't move into the fullness of our destiny because nobody likes adversity. We like to be comfortable. But you won't become all you were created to be without opposition, challenges, and difficulties that cause you to stretch and grow and use your spiritual muscles.

You're Going Through

When God brought the Israelites out of slavery, they were headed toward the Promised Land. God showed them their destination, the land flowing with milk and honey. He got them started on their way, brought them out of slavery, but in the middle God didn't abandon them. He didn't say, "I got you started. I gave you the promise and now you're on your own. Good luck in the middle." All along the way God supernaturally provided them with blessings. He gave them manna to eat in the desert. When they wanted meat, He caused the winds to shift and hundreds of thousands of quail came into the camp. When they were thirsty and couldn't find any streams or wells, God brought water out of a rock. He protected them from enemy nations that were much bigger and more powerful and trained for war. When Pharaoh came chasing after the Israelites, they came to a dead end at the Red Sea and had nowhere to go. God parted the sea and spared their lives. Again and again God gave them favor and made things happen that they could never have made happen. He was showing them and us, "I'm not just the God of the start, and I'm not just the God of the finish. I'm the God of the middle. I'm the God who will bring you through the trial, through the adversity, through the loss."

When you're in the middle, God has given you the promise, and you know the destination. But you're en route. You're in the process of raising your child, believing for your healing, or running that business. Along the way you'll face situations that look impossible—the odds are against you, the opposition is stronger, the report says you're not going to get well. Be encouraged, knowing that the God of the middle is right there with you. There may be a Red Sea in your path. It looks as though you're stuck, but the good news is, God knows how to part it. You may not have the funds for college, you don't see how you can go, but God is not lacking. He knows how to shift the winds and bring quail into your camp, so to speak. He can still bring water out of a rock. He can cause walls that have been stopping you to suddenly come tumbling down. Now do your part—have faith in the middle.

The Scripture says, "When you go through deep waters, I will be with you. When you go through the rivers, you will not drown. When you go through the fire, you won't be burned, the flames will not consume you." You may be in the fire, in the flood, or in the fam-

> *When you're in the middle, you need to remind yourself that this too shall pass. It's temporary.*

ine, but God is saying, "You're not staying there. You're going through it." When you're in the middle, you need to remind yourself that this too shall pass. It's temporary. Now quit putting so much energy into something that's not going to last. Quit wasting time by worrying about that situation at work, being upset over that medical report, or being frustrated with that person who did you wrong. That's not your destination; you're only passing through. The trouble is not permanent. The sickness, the loneliness, or the difficulty is just a stop along the way. But if you give in to it and let it overwhelm you with discouragement, you'll settle there and let what should have been temporary become permanent. This is where many people miss it—they settle in the middle. I'm asking you to keep moving forward.

David said it this way: "I walk through the valley of the shadow of death." He didn't say, "I stay in the valley. I set up camp in the valley. I build my house in the valley." He said, in effect, "The valley is not my home. I don't settle in the middle. I don't get discouraged when things come against me. I don't give up when it's hard, when life's not fair, when it's taking a long time. I have faith for the middle." When things come against you, and you're tempted to settle, you have to dig your heels in and say as David said, "I know that God is not just the God of the end. He's the God of the middle. And even though I may not understand it, I'm not going to settle in the valley. I'm not going to get stuck in the middle. I'm going to keep moving forward, knowing that God is in control and this difficulty is just another step on the way to my destiny."

You're Not Doing Life by Yourself

Psalm 138 says, "The Lord will work out His plans for my life." It doesn't say that we have to work out our plans, make things happen with our own strength, and be frustrated when they're not happening the way we thought they would. We can stay in peace, knowing that the Lord, the God who created the universe, the God who spoke worlds into existence, has promised He will work out His plans for our lives. Sometimes it feels as though we're going backward. We know we should be going one way, but we're going just the opposite way. God knows what He's doing. His ways are better than our ways. Right now He's behind the scenes working out His plans for your life. He's arranging things in your favor, moving the wrong people out of the way, lining up the breaks you need. You may not see anything happening; you have to walk by faith and not by sight.

In the middle, Joseph could have said, "It's never going to work out. I was a slave, and now I'm in prison in a foreign land. I'll never lead a nation." But what Joseph couldn't see was that behind the scenes God was working out the plan for his life. In the middle, David could have said, "I'll never take the throne. I'm a just a shepherd boy from a low-income family. I don't have the skills, the connections, or the training." But God is not dependent on what you don't have. When He breathed His life into you, He equipped you with everything you need. What you think you don't have enough of, the favor of God will make up for. The anointing on your life will take you further than people with more talent. In the middle, Abraham could have said, "Sarah and I will never have a baby. It's taking too long. We're way too old." But what Abraham couldn't see was that behind the scenes, God had already ordained a little baby named Isaac who had Abraham and Sarah's name on him. God already had it worked out for his life.

You may not be able to figure out how your dream can come to pass. When you put the business plan down on paper, it tells you that you won't get out of debt until you're a hundred years old. The medical report says you won't get well. It doesn't look as though you can ever break the addiction. On your own, you're out of luck. The good news is that you're not on your own. You're not doing life by yourself. Your Heavenly Father, the Most High God, is working out His plan for your life. There may be obstacles

> *The good news is that you're not on your own.*

that look insurmountable, but God has the final say. If you'll have faith in the middle, He'll open up doors that no man can shut. He'll turn situations around that look impossible. He'll take you further than you've ever imagined.

Days of Trouble Are Temporary

Paul said in Ephesians, "Put on the whole armor of God so that in the day of trouble you can stand." In life we'll all have days of trouble, days of difficulties, days of opposition, days of darkness. But the same God who said there will be a day of trouble has also said there will be a day when that trouble comes to an end. You may be in difficulty right now. Be encouraged—it's not permanent, that trouble has an expiration date. God has set an end to it. You're in the middle now, but at the appointed time, the end will come. Don't be overwhelmed by that sickness—it has an expiration date. That legal problem or that situation in your finances is not a surprise to God. It's one of those days of trouble. Instead of being discouraged, remind yourself, "This trouble has an end date." It's not permanent. Just as there is a day of trouble, God has a day of deliverance, a day of healing, a day of abundance, a day of breakthrough.

I know a couple who have a son who was addicted to drugs for over twenty years. These parents are good people who love God and are always serving and giving, but somehow their son got on the wrong track. Year after year went by, and it didn't look as though anything was changing. I never once heard these parents talk about the problem. They never complained, "God, why did this happen to our son? We don't understand it." They were in the valley, but they didn't stay there. They believed that just as there had been a day of trouble when their son got addicted, there would be a day of deliverance, set by the Creator of the universe, when their son would be free from that addiction. They did everything they could—they prayed, they believed, they sent him to rehab, but nothing worked. A few months ago, some people this young man worked with took a special interest in him. They weren't even believers, but they befriended the young man and went out of their way to help him. They paid his way through treatment, and this time it was successful. For the first time in more than twenty years, he's completely free. He has no desire for drugs.

What happened? He came into his day of deliverance. What his parents couldn't do, God caused somebody to do for him. When you have faith in the middle, God will make things happen that you can't make happen. You may be in a day of trouble now—in your health, in your finances, in your mind. It's easy to settle there and think, *It's never going to change. I'll never get free. I'll always be depressed. I'll always struggle in my finances.* But God is saying to you, as he said to this young man, "Your day of deliverance is coming. Your day of healing, your day of abundance, your day of blessing, your day of joy, your day of victory is on the way."

In Mark 4, Jesus had just finished teaching thousands of people. It was late in the day when He said to his disciples, "Let's go to the other side of the lake." They got in the boat and began to travel there, but along the way they were caught in a huge storm in the darkness of night. The Scripture describes it as a furious squall of winds, of hurricane proportions. The winds were so strong that the disciples thought the boat was going to capsize. Waves were coming over the top of it and the boat was filling up. They were in a panic. The disciples ran down to the stern of the boat where Jesus was sleeping. They said, "Jesus, wake up! We're about to drown in this huge storm!" Jesus woke up and rebuked the storm and said to the sea, "Peace, be still!" And everything calmed down.

What's interesting is that Jesus knew before they got on the boat that there was going to be a storm that night. He's God; He knows everything. Why did He suggest going to the other side if He knew there were going to be hurricane-force winds, a major storm? Because He also knew that that storm couldn't keep them from their destiny. He knew that in the middle there would be difficulties, but when He declares we're going to the other side, all the forces of darkness cannot stop Him from getting us to the other side. In the same way, when God puts a promise in your heart, when He speaks into your destiny, He's not moved by the winds. He's not worried by the storms or stressed out because there are a few hurricanes on your journey. He controls the universe. What He says will come to pass.

In the middle of that storm, Jesus didn't wake up on His own because He knew the disciples could handle it. If He'd thought they were going to die, He would have gotten up without their having to wake Him up. He wasn't going to let them all drown. When we're in a storm, we often get upset and panic as the disciples did. "God, You have to help me! This medical report is bad. My finances aren't making it. My relationship is falling apart. God, I have big things coming against me!" The reason it doesn't feel as though God is waking up is not that He's ignoring you or that He's uninterested. It's that He knows you can handle it. He wouldn't have let it come your way if it were going to sink you. He wouldn't have allowed that difficulty if it were going to stop your destiny.

Quit being upset over things you can handle. Quit losing sleep over that situation at work. Quit being panicked over that trouble. God is not ignoring you. He knew there would be a storm before He sent you out. He's not waking up because He's growing you up. He's teaching you to have faith in the middle. If He comes running every time you have a difficulty,

When you're calm despite what's coming against you, that's a sign of maturity. That's a sign that you've developed faith in the middle.

your spiritual muscles will never develop. You'll never really learn to trust Him. When you're calm despite what's coming against you, that's a sign of maturity. That's a sign that you've developed faith in the middle. If God has not turned it around yet, the winds are still blowing and the waves are still rocking, take it as a compliment. That means you can handle it. It's no match for you. You have the most powerful force in the universe on your side.

Don't Get Discouraged by the Process

Years ago, we were doing a Night of Hope in Dodger Stadium in Los Angeles. Our daughter, Alexandra, was a little girl at the time, and she would come up at the end of the program and sing. There were thousands of people there, and it was being broadcast live on television. She started her song, but the microphone wasn't working properly. It would come on for a second and go off for three seconds, cutting in and out. It's hard enough to sing in the stadium with all the echo, and now she couldn't hear herself. She didn't know what to do with so much confusion in her mind, every voice telling her, "Stop! Nobody can hear you!" She looked over to the left and could see Victoria sitting on the side of the platform. The whole time Victoria had a big smile on her face and was nodding, saying, "Keep going, keep going. You're doing good!" Alexandra would sing for another fifteen seconds, with the microphone cutting in and out. Then she would look back over, and there was Victoria still smiling and nodding. Alexandra made it through the whole song simply because she could see her mother reassuring her that everything was going to be all right.

Sometimes in life the microphone doesn't work. You're in the middle of your song. You thought it would be the best part of your life, but somebody walked away, the business didn't work out, or the medical report wasn't good. You hit one of those days of trouble. Every voice tells you to give up, it's not working, nobody can hear you. But if you'll look up through your eyes of faith, you'll see your Heavenly Father nodding, saying, "Keep going! I'm in control." When you're in the middle and the microphone quits working, the key is to just keep on singing. Keep on doing the right thing.

When you're in the middle and the microphone quits working, the key is to just keep on singing.

You can't control everything that happens to you. Just be your best and trust God to take care of the rest. He's not just the God of the start, not just the God of the finish; He's the God of the middle. He has you in the palms of His hands. Right now He's working out His plan for your life. Don't get discouraged by the process. You may be in the fire, but it's temporary. You're going to pass through it. If you'll have faith for the middle, I believe the God of the middle is going to protect you, provide for you, and favor you. You won't get stuck in the middle. He'll open doors that no man can shut and take you into the fullness of your destiny.

CHAPTER THIRTEEN

Anchored to Hope

An anchor is usually a metal device that is attached to a ship or boat by a cable and cast overboard to hold the ship in a particular place. Once the captain arrives at his destination, he puts the anchor down. That way he won't drift and end up where he doesn't want to be. When the boat is anchored, it may move a little bit with the waves and the winds, but the captain is not worried. He can relax, because he knows the anchor is down.

The Scripture tells us that hope is the anchor of our soul. What's going to keep your soul in the right place, what's going to cause you to overcome challenges and reach your dreams, is being anchored to hope. That means that no matter what you face, no matter how big the obstacle, no matter how long it's taking, you know God is still on the throne. You know His plans for you are for good, that He's bigger than any obstacle, and that His favor is surrounding you. When you are anchored to this hope, nothing can move you. The winds, the waves, and the dark storms of life may come, but you're not worried. You have your anchor down.

You receive a bad medical report, which would get a lot of people upset and negative, but not you. You're anchored to hope. "I know that God is restoring health to me." You go through a loss or a disappointment, and your emotions are pulling you toward bitterness and depression. But there's something that's holding you back. You can't explain it, but deep down you hear that voice saying, "Everything is going to be all right. God has beauty for these ashes." That's the anchor of hope. Maybe your dream looks impossible. You don't have the connections or the resources, and every voice says, "Give up! It's never going to happen. You're wasting your time." Most people would throw in the towel, but your attitude is, *I may not see a way, but I know God has a way. He's opening doors that no man can shut. Favor is in my future.* When you're anchored to hope, God will make things happen that you could never make happen.

But I've learned that there will always be something trying to get us to pull up our anchor—bad breaks, delays, disappointments. In these tough times, when life doesn't make sense, when your prayers weren't answered, when it's taking longer than you thought it would, you have to make sure to keep your anchor down. If you pull it up, you'll drift over into doubt, discouragement, and self-pity. When you're anchored to hope, it's as though you're tied to it. You can't go very far. You may have thoughts of doubt that say, "This problem is never going to work out." But your faith will kick in. "No, I know the answer is already on the way." On paper, it may tell you that it will take you thirty years to get out of debt. You could accept it, but because you're anchored to hope, there's something in you that says, "I know that God can accelerate it. I know that explosive blessings are coming my way." Your children may be off course, and it doesn't look as though they'll ever change.

> *When life doesn't make sense, when your prayers weren't answered, when it's taking longer than you thought it would, you have to make sure to keep your anchor down.*

You could become discouraged, but you're tied to hope. Every time those negative thoughts come, trying to pull you away, your anchor kicks in. "As for me and my house, we will serve the Lord."

My question is, do you have your anchor down? Do you have that hope, that expectancy that your dreams are coming to pass, that you're going to break that addiction, that your family is going to be restored? Or have you pulled up your anchor, and now you've drifted into doubt, mediocrity, not expecting anything good? Put your anchor back down. Scripture says, "Faith is the substance of things hoped for." You can't have faith if you don't first have hope. You have to believe that what God put in your heart will come to pass, that you will accomplish your dreams, that you'll meet the right people, that you'll live healthy and whole.

Be a Prisoner of Hope

One time David had a lot coming against him. He felt overwhelmed by life. Everything just kept getting worse. He was down and discouraged and had given up on his dreams. He was stuck in a very dark place. But then he finally said, "Why are you cast down, O my soul? Hope in the Lord." He realized that he'd let his circumstances cause him to pull up his anchor of hope. He said, in effect, "I'm going to put my anchor back down. I'm going to hope in the Lord."

You may not see any reason to be hopeful. It doesn't look as though you'll ever get well, ever get married, ever start that business. You have to do as David did and hope in the Lord. Don't put your hope in your circumstances; they may not work out the way you want. Don't put your hope in people; they may let you down. Don't put your hope in your career; things may change. Put your hope in the Lord, in the God who spoke worlds into existence, in the God who flung the stars into space. When you have your hope in Him, the Scripture says you'll never be disappointed. You may have some temporary setbacks, life will happen, but when it's all said and done, you'll come out better than you were before.

The prophet Zechariah said it this way: "Return to your fortress, you prisoners of hope, and I will restore double what you lost." To be a "prisoner of hope" means you can't get away from it. You're anchored to it. You should be discouraged, but in spite of all that's come against you, you still believe as Joseph did that you're going to see your dream come to pass. You should be overwhelmed by the size of the obstacles you are facing. Goliath looked stronger and more powerful, but like David, you have your hope in the Lord. You know that if God is for you, none will dare be against you.

> *"Return to your fortress, you prisoners of hope, and I will restore double what you lost."*

That sickness may seem as though it's going to be the end of you. You could be worried and feel stressed out, but you know nothing can snatch you out of God's hand. Your hope is not in the medicine, not in the treatment, not in the professionals, even though all those things are good and we're grateful for them. Your hope is in the Lord, in the God who breathed life into you. He's the God who makes blind eyes see. He's the God who caused a teenage shepherd boy to defeat a huge giant. He's the God who took Joseph from the darkness of the pit to the palace. He's the God who healed my mother of terminal cancer. I'm asking you to keep your anchor down. Keep your hope in the Lord.

When you find yourself being consumed by worry, full of doubt, thinking it's never going to work out, recognize what's happened. You've pulled your anchor up. The good news is that you can put it back down. Quit dwelling on the negative thoughts: *You'll never get well. You'll never get out of debt. You'll never meet the right person.* Turn it around and say, "Father, I thank You that the answer is on the way. Thank You that healing is coming, blessing is coming, freedom is coming, favor is coming, victory is coming." That's not just being positive; that's keeping your anchor down.

Hope On in Faith

This is what Abraham did. When God gave him a promise that he and his wife, Sarah, were going to have a baby, she was around seventy-five years old. It was impossible. It had never happened before. Abraham could have dismissed it and thought, *I must have heard God wrong*. I'm sure his friends said, "Abraham, you're an old man. Do you really think Sarah is going to have a baby at her age?" He could have talked himself out of it, but Scripture says, "All human reason for hope being gone, Abraham hoped on in faith."

> *"All human reason for hope being gone, Abraham hoped on in faith."*

Sometimes there's no logical reason to have hope. The medical report said that my mother would never get well. All the experts said that we'd never get the Compaq Center. Our opponents were much bigger and had more resources. There may be many reasons your situation will never work out. But you have to do as Abraham did—against all hope, hope on in faith. Don't pull your anchor up; don't get talked out of it. God is not limited by the natural. He's a supernatural God. Sarah was over ninety years old when she gave birth to a child. The promise was fulfilled, but they waited for fifteen years or so. It didn't happen overnight. There were plenty of times when they were tempted to think, *It's been too long. It's never going to happen. We're too old.* If they would have believed those lies, they would have drifted into doubt and discouragement and never seen the promise come to pass.

Are you drifting into doubt, worry, and negativity? I'm asking you to put your anchor down. Get your hopes up. Just because that promise hasn't been fulfilled yet doesn't mean it's not going to happen. You may have had some bad breaks like Joseph, but that doesn't mean you're not going to fulfill your destiny. If it weren't going to work for your good, God wouldn't have allowed it. Shake off the self-pity, shake off the disappointment. What God promised you, He's still going to bring to pass.

A young lady I know grew up in our church. She and her husband wanted to have a baby. They tried and tried and went through all the fertility treatments, with no success. Year after year went by. When my father went to be with the Lord and I became pastor, she was the head of our children's department. At that time she had already been believing to have this baby for over twenty years. We were in a meeting about the children's ministry, and she made the comment, "I have a good assistant trained, because when I have my baby, I'm going to be out for a little while." I thought I had missed something. Nobody had told me that she was pregnant. I asked my sister Lisa afterward if this young lady was going to have a baby. She said, "No, she's just believing to have one." She talked as though the baby were already on the way. She didn't say, "If I have a baby"; she said, "When I have my baby." What was that? She was anchored to hope.

I thought to myself, being the great man of faith that I am, *You've been believing for a baby for twenty years. It's time to move on. Maybe God wants to do it another way. Maybe you're supposed to adopt.* Don't let other people talk you out of what God put in your heart. Don't let them convince you to pull your anchor up. God didn't put the promise in them; He put the promise in you. That's why you can have faith when others think what you're believing for is far out. You can believe for it even though it seems impossible to them. This young lady kept her anchor down. Twenty-nine years after she started believing for a baby, she went to the doctor for a checkup. He said, "Congratulations, you're pregnant! And not with just one baby—you're pregnant with twins!" That's what Zechariah said: "If you'll stay anchored to hope, God will restore double what you lost."

What you're believing for may be taking a long time, but what God started He's going to finish. He doesn't abort dreams. Keep your anchor down.

Everyday Life Can Cause You to Drift

When I was a little boy, our family used to go to Galveston. I couldn't wait to get in the water and play in the waves. We'd find a place for our towels and shoes on the beach, then run out and start having fun in the water. After a couple of hours we were ready to take a break, and when we looked around for our towels, we realized we were a couple hundred yards down the beach from where we'd started. We hadn't known that that whole time we had been slowly drifting. The Scripture describes hope as the anchor of our soul. It wouldn't say "anchor" unless there was a possibility of drifting. This is what happens in life. If we don't keep our anchor down and stay full of hope, then little by little we start drifting, getting negative and discouraged. "I don't think I'll ever have a baby. It's been so long." "I'll never get well." "I'll never meet the right person." The problem is that you don't have your anchor down.

When you're anchored to hope, you may have negative circumstances, but you're not worried because you know that God is fighting your battles. You may not see how your dream can come to pass, but you don't give up. You know that God is behind the scenes arranging things in your favor. You may have a disappointment, but you don't get bitter. You know that weeping may endure for a night, but joy is coming in the morning. *Anchored to hope* doesn't mean you won't have difficulties; it means that when those difficulties come, you won't drift. Nothing will move you. Sure there will be waves, winds, and changing tides, but you're consistent—your hope is in the Lord.

What's interesting is that when we were at the beach, it wasn't a big storm or a hurricane or huge waves that caused us to drift. It was just the normal movement of the ocean. If you don't have your anchor down, the normal currents of life will cause you to drift. To drift does not require a major sickness, a divorce, or a layoff; just everyday life will do it. Perhaps you don't realize it, but you have drifted into a dark place of doubt. You're not believing for your dreams anymore. You used to be excited about your dreams, but it's been so long that you've lost your passion. Maybe you've drifted into bitterness

> *If you don't have your anchor down, the normal currents of life will cause you to drift.*

because you had a bad break, a person did you wrong. You used to be loving and kind, but now you're sour, not pleasant to be around. You used to believe that God was in control, knowing that He was taking care of you, but you pulled up your anchor and you've drifted into worry. Now you feel stressed out all the time. The good news is that you can get back to where you're supposed to be. You can put that anchor of hope down and start believing again, start expecting His goodness and blessings.

Life is too short for you to go through it drifting, feeling negative, discouraged, and passionless. Get your hopes back up. If you don't have an expectancy in your spirit that something good is coming, it will limit what God can do. The apostle Paul told Timothy to stir up his gifts. You have to stir up the hope. If you don't, you'll drift into self-pity, worry, and discouragement. "Well, Joel, if God is good, why haven't my dreams come to pass? Why did I have this bad break?" Because you have an enemy who's trying to keep you from your destiny. But here's the key: the forces that are for you are greater than the forces that are against you. Don't let what happens to you, big or small, cause you to pull up your anchor. If you'll keep your hope in the Lord, God will get you to where you're supposed to be.

Cut Any Anchor of Negativity

This is not just about being positive. Being hopeful is about your soul being anchored to the right thing, because if you're not anchored to hope, over time you'll become anchored to something else. You can become anchored to discouragement, where that's your default setting. You wake up discouraged and see everything with a tainted perspective. Everything is sour. It's because you're anchored to the wrong thing. I know people who are anchored to bitterness. They're so focused on who hurt them and what wasn't fair that bitterness has poisoned their whole lives. You can become anchored to self-pity and go around with a chip on your shoulder, always thinking about how unfair life has been. I'm not making light of what's happened. You may have a good reason to feel that way. I'm simply saying that being anchored to any of those things is going to keep you from your destiny. It's going to cause you to miss your purpose. It's time to cut that anchor and come over into hope. God didn't breathe His life into you, crown you with favor, and give you a royal robe so you could go around anchored to doubt, fear, and bitterness. He created you to be anchored to hope, to go out each day expecting His goodness, believing that the days ahead are better than the days behind.

When you face difficulties, keep the right perspective. A difficulty is not there to defeat you; it's there to promote you. David could have looked at Goliath and thought, *Oh man, I'll never defeat him. He's twice my size. I don't have a chance.* If David had taken up his anchor of hope, we wouldn't be talking about him. Goliath wasn't sent to stop David; he was sent to promote David. What you're facing is not meant to hold you back; it's meant to push you forward. Instead of being negative and saying, "God, why is this happening? How is it ever going to work out?" stay anchored to hope. "God, I don't see a way, but my hope is in You. I know that You have it all figured out, and You'll get me to where I'm supposed to be."

The Scripture says, "Hope deferred makes the heart sick." If you don't have hope that the problem is going to turn around, hope that the dream is going to work out, hope that the new house is in your future, or hope that your baby is on the way, then your heart, your spirit, is going to be sick. When you're not hopeful, positive, and expecting God's goodness, something is wrong on the inside. Even physically, when we feel stressed out and run down, our immune system is weakened. It won't fight off disease as it should. For your health's sake, keep the anchor of hope down. We all go through seasons in life when things aren't exciting. It's easy to have the blahs and lose our enthusiasm. That's part of the normal currents of life. Nobody lives on cloud nine with everything perfect and exciting every day. Part of the good fight of faith is to stay hopeful in the dry seasons. When it's taking a long time, keep a smile on your face and all through the day say, "Lord, thank You that You have good things in store." "Joel, what if I do that and nothing happens?" What if you do it and something does happen? I'd rather be anchored to hope than anchored to doubt, worry, and negativity. That's just going to draw in defeat.

One time a high school friend invited me to go fishing with him and his dad. We got in his boat and drove about an hour offshore and fished most of the morning. When we were finished and ready to come back home, he asked me to pull the anchor up. I pulled and pulled and couldn't get it up. His father came over, and we pulled together, but it would not budge. My friend cranked up the engine, a big powerful motor, and he started driving off really slowly, trying to force it to come loose. The anchor must have been caught under a big tree or rock, because when he tried to pull away, it pulled the boat backward and we almost tipped over. He circled the boat around to the other side and tried pulling it a different way, but the same thing happened. Finally his father got his big knife out and said, "This is all we can do." He cut the line. We left the anchor in the ocean. My friend didn't like losing his anchor, but the alternative was to be stuck out in the gulf.

Sometimes we're anchored to things that don't come up easily. If you've been anchored to discouragement, anchored to worry, or anchored to negativity for a long time, you may have to do as my friend's dad did and cut the line, so to speak. The enemy doesn't want you to be free. He doesn't want you to be anchored to hope. He wants you to go through life feeling sour, discouraged, and doubting. It's time to cut some lines. It's time to say, "This is a new day. I've been anchored to this junk long enough. I'm done with the negativity and the bitterness, living passionlessly and with no expectancy. I'm cutting those lines, and I'm anchoring myself to hope." You have to have the right perspective when dark times linger. That sickness can't defeat you. That addiction is only temporary. The right breaks are in your future. You

> *If you've been anchored to discouragement, anchored to worry, or anchored to negativity for a long time, you may have to do as my friend's dad did and cut the line, so to speak.*

may have had some disappointments, and life may have dealt you a tough hand, but that cannot stop your destiny. The odds may be against you, but the Most High God is for you. When you're anchored to hope, He'll show out in your life in ways you've never imagined.

Keep Your Anchor Down

I know a young man named Owen who's fifteen years old. His family attends our church. One of his favorite things to do was play basketball. He was always one of the best players on his team. His dream was to get a scholarship to play in college. He and his father were watching the 2014 NBA draft on television. There was a standout player from Baylor named Isaiah Austin who had been projected to go in the first round, but a few weeks before the draft he'd learned that he had a life-threatening disease called Marfan syndrome. It's a genetic disorder that weakens the connective tissues of the body, with the most serious complications involving the tissue that holds the heart muscles and blood vessels together so the body can grow and develop. If it's not treated, it can easily be fatal. It's very dangerous to play high-energy sports if you have this syndrome. Isaiah Austin was given a ceremonial draft pick that night, and the commentators gave a lot of descriptive facts about his career-ending disease.

Owen's father recognized all the same symptoms in Owen. He took Owen to the doctor, and he was also diagnosed with Marfan syndrome and told he could never play basketball again. His body couldn't support it. Sometimes life doesn't seem fair. Owen could have cut the line to his anchor of hope, given up on his dream, and lived bitter and sour. But Owen knew that that disappointment wasn't a surprise to God. His father said that when Owen was told the diagnosis, he cried for thirty seconds, but then he said, "Dad, I'm only thirteen. I can still become a coach, or a referee, or maybe even work for the NBA." Then Owen decided he wanted to help other kids like him, so he started having fund-raisers. In February 2016 he raised $140,000. I said that this young man needed to come work for us! Owen says, "You can make it your excuse, or you can make it your purpose."

> *"You can make it your excuse, or you can make it your purpose."*

Recently Owen had to have open heart surgery, a very serious procedure, to fix valves in his heart that were much too large. If they kept growing, they would burst like a balloon and cause instant death. One of the best surgeons for Marfan syndrome in the world lives here in Houston and operated on him. One day after the surgery, Owen was out of intensive care, and one week later, he left the hospital. One month later, he was back at church.

Friend, a bad break, a disappointment, a divorce, or a sickness can't stop you. When life throws you a curve, don't pull up your anchor. Do as Owen has done and keep hoping on in faith. You haven't seen your best days. God has you in the palms of His hands. It may have been meant for your harm, but He's going to use it for your good. If you'll stay anchored to hope, what is now your test will soon become your testimony. Like Owen, you will rise above every challenge, defeat every enemy, and become everything God created you to be.

CHAPTER FOURTEEN

Pushed into Your Purpose

We don't always understand why certain things happen to us. Maybe a friend you thought would be with you for years, somebody you counted on, suddenly moved away. Now you're having to find new friends. Or at work, you had all this favor, things were going great, but now there's conflict, everything is uphill, and you don't enjoy it. A friend of mine had been the sales manager at a large car dealership that was consistently breaking sales records, but not long ago the dealership was sold to a national company. His new supervisor didn't like him and treated him unfairly. My friend said, "After all these years, I never dreamed I would have to be looking for another job."

Sometimes God will let us be uncomfortable for a dark, difficult period so He can bless us later on. He'll close a door, which we don't like and don't understand, but later on He'll open a bigger door. He'll take us to a new level of our destiny. God is not as concerned about our comfort as He is about our purpose. There are times when He will shake things up—a friend will do you wrong, the business will slow, you'll lose a loved one. God will use persecution, rejection, and loss to force us to change. His goal is not to make our life miserable; He's pushing us into our purpose.

Not every closed door is a bad thing. Not every time a person walks away from us is a tragedy. God knows we won't move forward without a push. When everything is going well, we're comfortable. We don't want to stretch, or to find a new friend, or to develop new skills. To step out into the unknown can be scary. What if it doesn't work out? We may not like it, but if God had not shut that door, we would have been satisfied to stay where we were. God loves you too much to let you miss your destiny.

> *You have too much potential, too much talent, too much in you for you to get stuck where you are.*

You have too much potential, too much talent, too much in you for you to get stuck where you are. He'll put you in situations that make you stretch, make you grow, make you spread your wings.

None of the difficulties you've gone through, none of the bad breaks you've experienced, and none of the times when someone hurt you were meant to stop you. They were meant to push you, to stretch you, to mature you, to make you stronger. They deposited something inside you. It's made you into who you are today. You wouldn't be prepared for the new levels if you had not been through what you've been through. Don't complain about the person who did you wrong, the loved one you lost, or the job that didn't work out. That was all a part of God's plan. When you face a difficulty, something you don't understand, instead of being discouraged, instead of complaining, have a new perspective. *This is not here to defeat me; it's here to promote me. I may not like it, and I may be uncomfortable, but I know that God is using it to push me to a new level, to push me to greater influence, to push me into my purpose.*

A Closed Door Means a New Door Will Open

When I look back over my life, I can see the pivotal moments when I really grew, the times when I stepped up to a new level. The common denominator was that I was pushed. At the time I didn't like it, and I was uncomfortable. I wanted to stay where I was. I wouldn't have done it on my own. God had to shut the doors and force me to take steps of faith. He pushed me into my purpose.

When I was nineteen years old, I came back from college to start a television ministry for my father at Lakewood. That was always my passion—television production, editing, cameras, etc. I was young and had a lot of enthusiasm, but I didn't have much training. We hired a seasoned television producer who was in his sixties. He had produced the *Today* show for years, then gone on to production work with Major League Baseball. He was not only very talented, but he was also very friendly. He and I hit it off. For one year I was with him night and day, and I was excited to be learning so much. I watched him during the services as he directed the cameras, and he taught me what the right angles were, what good lighting looked like, and how to edit. As I watched him make all those decisions, I would think, *How in the world does he know how to do all that?* I was amazed by him and so glad that we had him.

One morning about a year after he started, he came in and said, "Joel, I'm going to move back to California. I've done everything I need to do. You can take it from here." I almost passed out. I said, "You have to be kidding. You can't leave us.

What are we going to do? Who's going to direct the program? Who's going to edit it?" He said, "You are. You can do everything I'm doing. I've trained you for a year." I told him that there was no way. I didn't know how to do it. We offered him more money and more time off. I said, "You can live in California and just come in twice a month." I tried my best, but he said, "No, my time here is done." I was so disappointed. I thought that was the worst thing in the world that could happen. I prayed night and day, "God, please change his mind. Please don't let him go. God, You know this television ministry is going to fall apart."

Sometimes we're praying against the very thing that God has ordained, against what He set into motion. The enemy doesn't close every door. Sometimes God closes the door. He moves people out of our life because He knows they will become a crutch and keep us from our potential. God will cause a situation to dry up, so we'll be forced to change. My friend left and went back to California. I had to get out of my comfort zone, stretch, and start doing things I'd never thought I could do. As I stepped out, I discovered it wasn't as hard as I'd thought. The first month went by and I thought, *I'm not too bad at this*. Six months went by and I thought, *I'm pretty good at this*. A year went by and I thought, *What did we ever need him for?*

His leaving was a turning point in my life. God used that to push me into my destiny. Even though I was uncomfortable, it was the best thing that could have happened to me. If he had stayed, it would have stunted my growth. I wouldn't be who I am today if God had answered my prayer. Quit being sad over somebody who walked away.

> *The closed door means you're about to be pushed into your purpose—you're about to see new growth, new talents, new opportunities.*

If they left you, their time was up. Step into the new season. If the door closed and you went through a disappointment, don't go around complaining. The closed door means you're about to be pushed into your purpose—you're about to see new growth, new talents, new opportunities.

Out of Your Comfort Zone

The prophet Samuel had spent years mentoring King Saul as a young man and loved him like a son. But Saul wouldn't do what was right as the king, and God told Samuel that He was going to take the throne away from Saul. Samuel was discouraged and felt as though he had wasted all that time. God said to Samuel, "Quit weeping over what I've rejected." God is saying to us, "Quit being depressed over who left your life. Quit being sour over what didn't work out." If they were supposed to be there, they would still be there. God told Samuel, "I've found a new man. His name is David, and I want you to go anoint him as the next king." Notice the principle: if you'll quit being discouraged over who left, the right people will show up. But that won't happen if you keep complaining about the Sauls in your life and what didn't work out. If I had said, "The veteran television producer left me here, and I can't do this production on my own," that would have caused me to get stuck. When you accept what has happened and move forward, not only is that going to push you to a new level, but the Davids are going to show up. The people you need will be there for each season of your life.

For seventeen years I did the television production. I thought that was how I would spend the rest of my life. I loved doing it. I was content. But in 1999 my father went to be with the Lord, and again I was forced to change. God shut another door in my life. In the Old Testament, Job said, "I thought I would die in my nest." He was saying that he'd had his nest all fixed up, had his house just as he wanted it, and had a successful business. Things were going great. He was finally comfortable, but what happened? God stirred up his nest. God doesn't bring the trouble, but He will allow difficulties to push us into our destiny. Job went through all kinds of challenges. Almost overnight he lost his health, his children, and his business. If the story stopped there, it would be a sad ending. But Job understood this principle. In spite of all the difficulty, he said, "I know my Redeemer lives." He was saying, "I know God is still on the throne, and He has the final say. This trouble is not going to defeat me; it's going to push me." In the end Job came out with twice what he'd had before. When you get comfortable and think you have your life figured out, as Job did and as I did, don't be surprised if God comes along and stirs things up. It's not to harm you; it's to push you. God has new levels in your destiny, more influence and more resources for you. His dream for your life is greater than you imagine.

I knew that I was supposed to pastor the church. But just as with the production, I didn't think I could do it. I didn't have the training or the experience. My father had tried to get me up in front for years, but I was comfortable behind the scenes. I didn't have to stretch anymore; I could do the production in my sleep. Like Job, I thought I would die in my nest, but when my father went to be with the Lord, it was as though the whole process started over. That loss pushed me out of my comfort zone, pushed me to discover new talents, pushed me into greater influence. Every time I've seen major

Every time I've seen major growth in my life, every time I've stepped up to a new level, it happened because I was pushed.

growth in my life, every time I've stepped up to a new level, it happened because I was pushed. It involved adversity, loss, and disappointment. You may be in a situation where you could easily be discouraged—you lost a loved one, you went through a breakup, your business didn't work out. The enemy may have meant that for harm, but God is going to use that to your advantage. God wouldn't have allowed it if it were going to stop you. He allowed it so it can push you. Just as with Job, He's going to bring you out increased, promoted, stronger, wiser, and better than you were before. That sickness is going to push you into your purpose. That bad break is going to push you into something greater. That betrayal is going to push you into new happiness.

The pain is a sign that you're about to birth something new. The greater the difficulty, the closer you are to the birth. It's easy to think that a loss is the end, but you'll discover that it's going to birth you into a new level of your destiny, just as loss did for me. The disappointment, the persecution, or the betrayal may be painful, and you may not like it, but if you'll stay in faith, it's going to promote you. I wouldn't be where I am today if God had not taken that man away and pushed me when I was twenty years old. I wouldn't be leading the church today if He hadn't pushed me when my father died in 1999. That was difficult, but God doesn't waste the pain. The pain is a sign of new birth.

The Nest Will Be Stirred Up

Steve Jobs was one of the most brilliant minds of our generation. At twenty-one years old, he cofounded Apple Computer with Steve Wozniak. By the time he was twenty-three, he was incredibly successful and known around the world. But at thirty years old, after creating this global brand and developing so many great products, he clashed with his board of directors and eventually was forced out of the company he'd started. He told his friends how betrayed he felt and how wrong it was. But he didn't sit around in self-pity, thinking about what hadn't worked out. He went out and started another company and learned new skills.

This new company created something that Apple needed. It was so successful that Apple bought it and brought him back as Apple's CEO, and he is credited with revitalizing the company. He said, "Getting fired from Apple was the best thing that could have ever happened to me.... It freed me to enter one of the most creative periods of my life."

That betrayal wasn't sent to stop you; it was sent to push you. Don't complain about who did you wrong and how unfair it was. If it were going to keep you from your destiny, God would not have permitted it. Shake off the self-pity and get ready for new doors to open, for new opportunities, new skills, new friendships. Moses said, "As an eagle stirs up its nest, so God will stir up His children." When things are stirring in your life, when things are uncomfortable and you don't get your way—a door closes, a friend betrays you—don't think, *Well, that's just my luck. I never get any good breaks.* Turn it around and say, "God, I know You're in control and You're stirring up things because You're about to open up new doors, You're about to take me to a higher level, You're about to push me into my purpose."

I was in the hospital room when Victoria was giving birth to both of our children. I was right by the bed, and she had ahold of my arm. When

When you're being pushed, don't be discouraged. Rather be encouraged; it's the right time. Get ready, for something good is coming your way.

she had a contraction, it was very painful for both of us. She would squeeze my arm very tightly, then she would finally give a scream, and I would scream. The greater the pain, the closer she was to giving birth. At one point the doctor told her, "When you have a contraction, I want you to push." He didn't have her push until the birth canal was open and the baby was ready to come. In the same way, when you're being pushed, that means the door is open. Something new is coming—new levels, new influence, new growth. God wouldn't be pushing if the door were closed and nothing good were in store. Doctors don't tell women who are in labor, "Just push whenever you feel like it." That doesn't do any good. They have to wait for the right time. When you're being pushed, don't be discouraged. Rather be encouraged; it's the right time. Get ready, for something good is coming your way.

Consider that while a little baby is in the womb for nine months, everything is great. He's comfortable. He doesn't have to do anything. He gets his food from his mother, gets carried around all day, and sleeps whenever he wants. He's calm and peaceful. Life is good. For a season that's healthy. He's growing and developing. That's where he's supposed to be. But if he stays in the womb too long, instead of the womb being a blessing, it will be a burden. At a certain point it's too small and will keep him from his destiny and limit his potential. He has to get out. When he comes through the birth canal, it's tight, uncomfortable, and traumatic. All he's known up to this point is peace, lying around, having everything done for him. Suddenly it's as though all hell breaks loose. He thinks, *What in the world is Mama doing? Has she lost her mind? Doesn't she love me?* He's being pushed, squeezed, pressured, then more pushing, more pushing, and finally he comes out and is born. He breathes new life and enters a new level.

It's the same principle with us: when things get tight, when we're uncomfortable and feel pressure, it's easy to think, *What's happening? It was so peaceful. I want to go back to how it was.* But if you stay in the womb, that protected place, too long, it won't be a blessing; it will be a curse. It will keep you from becoming what you were created to be. God controls the universe. He knows what's best for you. If you're being pushed, it's because a door is open. God has something greater in your future, and you're about to step into a new level. You're about to tap into gifts and talents that you didn't know you had. It may be uncomfortable, but don't complain. God is stretching you, He's enlarging you. You're about to see new growth, new talents, new opportunities.

A Push Down Is a Push Up

I mentioned in chapter seven that my father pastored a denominational church for many years. At one point he started telling his congregation that God wanted them to live a victorious, overcoming life. This new message didn't fit into their tradition. Some of his longtime friends, people my parents had known for thirty years, turned on them and started stirring up trouble and said that he needed to leave. My father was devastated. He thought, *I've given my life to these people. God, why is this happening?* But the fact is, God was the one stirring it up. God knew my father would never reach his full potential in that limited environment. It felt like a huge disappointment, but behind the scenes God was orchestrating it all. God wouldn't push you if he didn't have another door open.

My father resigned from that church feeling rejected and betrayed. But he didn't sink into self-pity or go around talking about how bad life was. He understood this principle: he was being pushed into his purpose. He realized the same God who opens doors closes doors. He went out and started Lakewood Church with ninety people in 1959, and here we are today still going strong. Had those people never been against him, he would never have reached his highest potential. Don't get upset with the people who do you wrong, betray you, or leave you out. God uses people to push you to where you're supposed to be. Without them you couldn't fulfill your destiny. They may think they're pushing you down, but what they don't realize is that they're pushing you up.

The Scripture says, "Persecution arose in Jerusalem...so Philip went down to the city of Samaria." It doesn't say that Philip prayed about it and decided that he was going to Samaria. He didn't have a choice. The persecution forced him out of his hometown of Jerusalem. He was pushed out of his comfort zone. What's interesting is that previously in Jerusalem, God had poured out His Spirit upon the believers in the upper room. The same God who showed them that great sign could have taken care of the persecution. God could have stopped the opposition. He closed the mouths of hungry lions for Daniel. It would have been no big deal, but the persecution was for a purpose. The opposition was a part of God's plan to push them into their destiny. It was in Samaria that Philip saw the greatest days of his ministry. If he had stayed in Jerusalem, he would never have reached his full potential. Maybe you've been pushed out of Jerusalem, so to speak, through a bad break, a disappointment, a betrayal.

> *Don't be discouraged. Jerusalem may have closed, but Samaria is about to open.*

Don't be discouraged. Jerusalem may have closed, but Samaria is about to open. God wouldn't be pushing you if He didn't already have a door open.

A friend of mine was working at a job, but he wasn't fulfilled. He knew he had outgrown what he could do there. He had much more in him, but he was afraid to take a step of faith. This man is one of the nicest people you'll ever meet, very kind, easygoing. He's a model employee, always fifteen minutes early, and never breaks the rules. He called me one day and said, "Joel, you'll never believe what just happened." I said, "What?" He said, "I just got fired." I said, "You got fired!" It was like saying, "Mother Teresa just robbed a bank!" It was so hard to believe. But God loved him too much to let him stay in mediocrity. God knows how to get you out of your comfort zone. He opened the door; He can close the door. If we don't take the hint, He'll push us. Today that man is a vice president at a major company. He continues to rise higher. Don't complain about the closed doors. That's God pushing you. Don't be discouraged by the bad break. If it weren't going to work for your good, God wouldn't have allowed it.

Go through the Process

In the Scripture, God told the apostle Paul that he was going to stand before Caesar. He was on a boat headed toward Rome when they encountered a huge storm. The winds were so strong that they finally drove the ship aground. The boat was broken up by the violent waves, and all who were aboard the ship had to swim to a small island called Malta. It looked as though Paul's plans hadn't worked out. It was a bad break, a disappointment, but that storm didn't stop God's plan; it was a part of God's plan. It blew Paul into his purpose. On that island the chief official's father was very sick. Paul prayed for him, and the man was healed. They brought other sick people, and they too were healed. Paul ended up sharing his faith with the people on that whole island, and many came to know the Lord.

What am I saying? God will use the winds that were meant to harm you to push you into your

> *That storm is not going to defeat you; it's going to promote you. The storm blew my father from a limited environment to a church that touched the world.*

destiny. You may not understand, it may be uncomfortable, but keep the right attitude. That storm is not going to defeat you; it's going to promote you. The storm blew my father from a limited environment to a church that touched the world. It blew my friend from a job where he wasn't using his gifts to the vice presidency of a large company. It blew me from being behind the scenes into the position I'm in now. You're being pushed for a reason. There's something bigger, something better, something more rewarding up in front of you.

You have to be willing to go through the process. When you feel pressured, when it's tight and you're being squeezed, that's because you're about to see a birth. Where you are is too small. The womb was good for a time and served its purpose, but now you're coming into a season of new growth, new opportunity, and new talents. Have the right perspective. Say, "This sickness is not going to stop me; it's pushing me, and I'm coming out better." "This trouble at work is not going to hold me back; it's pushing me." "The people who did me wrong can't stop my destiny. They meant it for harm, but they don't realize that God is using it for good. It's pushing me."

Every storm you went through, every bad break, and every dark, lonely season deposited something on the inside. It pushed you to mature, pushed you to trust God in a greater way, pushed you to be more resilient and determined. Don't get discouraged by the process. Perhaps you are being pushed right now—you're being squeezed, pressured, and it feels uncomfortable. You need to get ready, you're about to see new birth. If you'll keep the right attitude, God is about to push you to a new level. He's going to push you into greater influence, greater strength, greater resources. You're coming into a new season of health, favor, abundance, promotion, and victory. Those winds that were meant to stop you are going to push you into your purpose.

CHAPTER FIFTEEN

Step into the Unknown

When I type an address into my navigation system, one of the options that comes up is "Route Overview." When I click on that, it gives me all the details of my trip. There may be fifteen different instructions. "Travel six miles on the highway, get off at Exit 43, go four hundred feet, turn left at the intersection." Your whole route is clearly laid out. You know where you're going, how long it's going to take, and what to expect. Knowing all the details makes us comfortable. We can relax.

In a similar way, God has a route overview for your life. Before you were formed in your mother's womb, He laid out your plan. He not only knows your final destination, He knows the best way to get you there. But unlike the navigation system, God doesn't show you the route overview. He doesn't tell you how it's going to happen, how long it's going to take, where the funds are going to come from, or whom you're going to meet. He leads you one step at a time. If you'll trust Him and take that step into the unknown, not knowing how it's going to work out, He'll show you another step. Step-by-step, He'll lead you into your destiny.

The difficulty of this method is that we like details. We wouldn't have any problem with taking that step of faith—starting that business, going back to school, moving to that new location—if we knew where the money was coming from, how long it was going to take, and that the right people were going to be there for us. If we had the details, it would be easy to step out. But here's the key: God doesn't give the details. He's not going to give you a blueprint for your whole life. If you had all the facts, you wouldn't need any faith. He's going to send you out not knowing everything. If you'll have the courage to step into the unknown and do what you know He's asking you to do, doors will open that you could never have opened, the right people will show up, you'll have the funds and any other resources you need.

The Scripture says, "Your word is a lamp to my feet and a light to my path." "A lamp" implies you have enough light to see right in front of you. He's not giving you the light that shows your life for the next fifty years. It's more like the headlights of a car. When you're driving at night, with your low beam headlights you can only see a hundred feet or so in front of you. You don't stop driving because you can't see your destination, which is twenty-five miles ahead. You just keep going, seeing as much as the lights allow, knowing you'll eventually arrive at your destination.

My question is, will you take the next step that God gives you with the light you have? If you're waiting for all the details, you'll be waiting your whole life. We all want to be comfortable, but walking in God's perfect will is going

> *If you're waiting for all the details, you'll be waiting your whole life.*

to make you a little uncomfortable. There's a healthy tension: you have to stretch, you have to pray, and you have to believe. You're not going to be sure how it's all going to work out, but that is what will cause you to grow, that's when you'll learn to trust God in a greater way. God is not interested only in the destination. He's teaching you along the way; He's getting you prepared and growing you up. He will lead you purposefully into situations where you're in over your head, your friends can't help you, and you don't have the experience you think you need. Too often we shrink back and think, *I'm not going there. I'm not qualified. I'm too nervous. What if it doesn't work out?* God knew that you would be nervous, and He knew that you would feel unqualified. That's a test.

Are you going to talk yourself out of it? Are you going to let the fear of what you can't see hold you back? Or are you going to be bold and step into the unknown? The unknown is where miracles happen. The unknown is where you discover abilities that you never knew you had. The unknown is where you'll accomplish more than you ever dreamed. Just because you don't have the details doesn't mean God doesn't have the details. He has the route overview for your whole life. He wouldn't be leading you there if He didn't have a purpose. He has the provision, He has the favor, and He has what you need to go to the next level.

You'll Have to Be Bold

One thing I like about my navigation system is that it gives me specific details. "Go 9.3 miles down this freeway and exit at..." The whole time it counts down—eight miles left, seven miles, six miles. It's all right in front of me to see.

But God does not direct us that way. He'll tell

you to go down a certain road. Then the first thing we do is ask for details. "How far do You want me to go?" No answer. "Where do You want me to turn?" No answer. "What's the weather going to be like?" No answer. "Who's going to meet me?" No answer. It would be so much easier if God would give us specifics. But that wouldn't take any faith. Can you endure the silence of not knowing everything? Will you trust God even though you don't have the details? Will you take that step of faith even though you're nervous, uncomfortable, and not sure how it's going to work out?

This is what Abraham did. God told him to leave the place where he was living and go to a land He would show him. Abraham was to pack up his household, leave his extended family behind, and head out to a land that God was going to give him as his inheritance. The only problem was that God didn't give him any details. The Scripture says, "Abraham went out, not knowing where he was going." I can imagine Abraham telling his wife, Sarah, "Honey, I've got great news. We're going to move. God promised me He's taking us to a better land where we're going to be blessed in a new way." I can hear Sarah saying, "That's so exciting! I can't wait.

> *"Abraham went out, not knowing where he was going."*

Where are we going?" Abraham answers, "I'm not sure. He didn't tell me." She asks, "What should I wear? Will it be hot or cold?" He answers, "I don't know." At that point, reality sets in for Sarah, who responds, "Well, Abraham, how are we going to make a living? Where are we going to get food for our children and staff? This seems like a mistake. Are you sure that God told you this?"

If you're going to step into the unknown, it's going to take boldness. It's not always going to make sense. Other people may not understand. They may try to talk you out of it. Your own thoughts will tell you, *You better play it safe. This is too big a risk. What if it doesn't work out?* Abraham understood this principle; he knew that just because you don't have all the answers, and just because you're nervous and uncomfortable, doesn't mean you aren't supposed to do it. The psalmist said, "The steps of a good person are ordered by the Lord." If you'll take that step, not knowing all the details but trusting that God knows what He's doing, then each step of the way there will be provision, there will be favor, there will be protection. Yes, it's uncomfortable not knowing the details; and yes, you have to stretch, you have to pray, and you have to trust. But every step you'll not only have God's blessing; you'll also be growing and getting stronger.

It Is Possible to Walk on the Water

In the Scripture, when Jesus came walking across the stormy sea in the darkness of night, Peter was the only disciple to walk on the water to Him. He also was the only one who had the courage to get out of the boat in the first place. I can imagine the other disciples saying, "Peter, you better stay in here with us! The waves are big. It's too dangerous. You could drown." But when Jesus told him to come, Peter stepped out into the unknown and walked on the water. "Well, Joel, you failed to note that he sank." Yes, but he walked on the water more than you or I have. Although what is familiar is comfortable, it can become a curse rather than a blessing. Familiarity—what you're used to, how you were raised, the job you've had for years—can keep you from your destiny. Don't let your comfort keep you from getting out of the boat and becoming who you were created to be.

If Abraham had put his comfort above fulfilling his purpose, we wouldn't be talking about him. It was a risk to pack up his family and leave, not knowing where he was going. You can't play it safe your whole

You can't play it safe your whole life and reach the fullness of your destiny.

life and reach the fullness of your destiny. Don't
let the what-ifs talk you out of it. "What if I fail?
What if I don't have the funds? What if they say
no?" You'll never know unless you try. When you
come to the end of your life, will you have more
regrets about the risks you took or about the risks
you didn't take? "What if I start a new business
and it fails?" What if you start it and it thrusts
you to a new level? "What if I get into this new
relationship and I get hurt again? That's what happened last time." What if you get into it and you're
happier than you've ever been? What if it's a divine
connection? "What if I take this new position and
I'm not good at it? What if I'm not successful?"
What if you take it and you excel? What if you
discover new gifts you didn't know you had? What
if it leads you to more opportunities?

For every major victory and every significant
accomplishment in my life, I've had to step into
the unknown. When my father went to be with
the Lord and I stepped up to pastor the church,
I didn't know how it was going to work out. I
didn't know if I could minister. I didn't know if
anyone would listen to me. Every voice said, "Don't
do it! You're making a mistake. You're going to
get up there and look like a fool." I knew I was
going in over my head, and I knew I didn't have
the experience. But I also knew that when we are

weak, God's power shows up the greatest. I couldn't see very far down the road. I couldn't see anything of what we're doing today. All I could see was this much: "Joel, step up and pastor the church." If God had shown me all that we're doing today and what it would take to get here, I would have said, "No way. I can't do that." Sometimes the reason God doesn't tell us what's in our future is that He knows we can't handle it right then.

What God has in store for you is going to boggle your mind—the places He's going to take you, the people you're going to influence, the dreams you're going to accomplish. It's going to be bigger than you've imagined. You know where it is—it's in the unknown, in what you can't see right now, in what you don't feel qualified for, in what looks way over your head. When you have something in front of you that seems too big and you don't think you have what it takes to do it, that's God stretching you. He sees things in you that you can't see. You may be uncomfortable, but don't shrink back. Keep stretching, keep praying, and keep believing. You're growing. God is leading you step-by-step. You are about to step into the next level. You've been on that step you're on for long enough. You've passed that test, and now the next step is coming—a new level of favor, a new level of blessing, a new level of influence, a new level of anointing.

Take the Step of Faith

Victoria and I were driving to another city not long ago. I had my navigation system on. At one point we were on a country road for about a hundred-mile stretch. There were so many intersections where roads veered off from it. I was concerned that I had missed my turn. I had to keep looking to make sure that I was okay. I noticed that as long as I was on the right path, the voice of the GPS was silent. I wished she would come on and say, "You're doing good. Keep going. You're right on track." But she never said a thing until it was time to do something different. Sometimes God is silent. You don't hear Him saying anything. It's easy to think you must be off course, something must be wrong. He's not talking. But as with the GPS, that means you're on the right course. Keep being your best with what you have. Keep stretching, praying, and believing. The next step is coming. You have to pass the test of being faithful where you are. That next step is going to be an increase step, a favor step, a healing step, a breakthrough step.

In the Scripture, when Joshua and the Israelites came to the Jordan River, there was no way for them to get across. The people had heard how Moses had held up his rod and the Red Sea had parted many years before. I'm sure that Joshua thought that if he did the same thing, the waters would part for him. But God had a different plan. He told Joshua to have the priests who were carrying the ark of the covenant step into the river; then the waters of the Jordan would part. I can imagine the priests saying, "Joshua, you want us to walk into the water? That doesn't make sense. We could drown in those dark waters." They got to the shore and nothing happened. They got to the banks a few feet away and still nothing. Thoughts started telling them, *What if it doesn't part? What if Joshua made a mistake? What if we get out there and can't get back?* They could have talked themselves out of it, but instead they dared to step into the unknown. The Scripture says that the moment their feet touched the edge of the waters, the water upstream began piling up while the water on the other side flowed downstream. It wasn't long till the riverbed was empty and they were able to walk across on dry land.

Notice that the miracle happened along the way. We think, *God, when You part the river, I'll go.* God says, "Go, and I'll part the river." If you'll step into the unknown, along the way you'll see miracles, doors

> *If you'll step into the unknown, along the way you'll see miracles, doors will open that you couldn't open, and the right people will show up.*

will open that you couldn't open, and the right people will show up. God could have just as easily parted the water first, before the priests stepped in. He was showing them and us this principle: when you don't see how it can work out, when you don't know where the funds are coming from, when every thought tells you to play it safe, but you take that step of faith and do what God has put in your heart, you're showing God that you trust Him. That's when Jordan Rivers will part. God will purposefully put us in situations where we can't do it on our own and it looks impossible—that's a test of our faith. If you stay in the boat, you'll never walk on the water. You'll never see the fullness of your destiny. If God had parted the water before the Israelites stepped into it, it would have been a lot less stressful. They wouldn't have had to pray and believe and stretch. But here's the key: God uses the journey to get us prepared for where we're going. When we have to stretch our faith, believe that He's making a way, and thank Him that things are turning in our favor, that is strengthening our spiritual muscles. We're developing a greater confidence in God.

The Purpose Is to Prepare You

In chapter six, I wrote about the Compaq Center. I didn't know how complicated it would be to acquire it. I had to step into the unknown. It was a city-owned facility. The mayor was a friend of our family. I called him, and he was in favor of our purchasing it. That was the first miracle. We needed ten votes from city council members, and we had only nine, but the night before the main vote, after two years of opposing us, a council member changed his mind and decided to vote for us. We got the building! Another miracle. A week later, however, a company filed a lawsuit to try to prevent us from moving in. We were told that it could be tied up in the courts for up to ten years. I had already told the church the building was going to be ours, and people had given money. I would wake up in the dark of night sweating, with thoughts telling me, *This is going to be a big mess. You're going to look like a fool. You have to give those funds back.* But as happened for Joshua, along the way miracles kept happening. The CEO of that opposing company eventually flew in from out of town. Our lawyers told us it was a ploy to try to confuse things. He said, "Joel, I watch you on television, and my son-in-law is a youth pastor. Let's work something out." Two days later, the lawsuit was dropped. We were on our way. When you go out not knowing where you're going, God will make things happen that you could never make happen. You'll see Jordan Rivers part, you'll see Compaq Centers fall into place, you'll see the surpassing greatness of God's favor. Don't stay in the boat. Don't let the fact that you can't see all the details hold you back. You're not supposed to see it all. God is leading you step-by-step.

When you're in the unknown, when you're stretching, praying, and believing, that's when you're really growing. The journey is more important than the destination. Why? Because if you're not prepared during the journey, if you don't learn what you're supposed to learn along the way, you won't be able to handle where God is taking you. God could have given us the Compaq Center in the first week we prayed, or at least the first month. That would have saved me a lot of stress, a lot of praying, and a lot of believing. Why did He wait three years? He was getting me prepared. I was learning to trust Him, my faith was being increased, and my character was being developed.

It's interesting that during those three years, as with the silence of the lady who voices the GPS, I didn't hear anything new. I didn't hear God say,

"You're doing good, Joel. Be patient. It's all going to work out. I've got you covered." I had to trust Him when He was silent. I had to believe that He was in control even when I didn't see any sign of it. I had to keep reminding myself that the steps of a good person are ordered by the Lord. I took my steps knowing that God had put the dream in my heart. I didn't know how it would work out. I didn't know if we would be successful, but I believed that I was doing what God wanted us to do.

> *I had to trust Him when He was silent.*

Here's the thing: even if you miss it, even if doesn't work out the way you thought, God knows how to use it for your good. God would rather you take a step of faith and miss it every once in a while than play it safe all the time and never make a mistake. Sometimes the mistakes, the closed doors, and the times we miss it are parts of God's plan. They're preparing us for the next open door. But if you're concerned that you're going to miss the next step, you'll never get off dead center.

The Not-Knowing Factor

Too many times we let the fear of the unknown hold us back. When you're in God's will, there's going to be a not-knowing factor. You're not going to know all the details about how it's going to work out or where the funds are going to come from. If you're going to reach your highest potential, you have to have the boldness to step into the unknown.

My brother, Paul, is a medical doctor. For seventeen years he was the chief of surgery at a hospital in Arkansas and had a very successful practice. It looked as though that's how he would spend his life. But when my father went to be with the Lord in 1999, he felt God leading him to come back and help us pastor the church. His colleagues told him that he was having a midlife crisis. They said that he should wait a couple of years in order to get over our father's death and not make an emotional decision. But deep down Paul knew what he was supposed to do, even though leaving his medical practice and all that training didn't make sense to his mind. Thoughts asked him, *What if it doesn't work out? What if you don't like it? What if they don't like you? What if you get back there and Joel makes fun of you?* In the natural it looked as though he were making a mistake, but as Abraham did, Paul went out, not knowing how it was going to work out. He didn't have all the details. We didn't come up with a ten-year strategy. All he knew was that first step: "Go help your family."

What Paul didn't know was how the ministry was

going to grow. He didn't know that after eight years of his being faithful in the pastoring of the church, God would open the door for him to go to Africa for several months a year and operate on people. Paul's dream had been to do medical missions, but he'd thought he was giving up medicine completely. What he couldn't see was that it was all a part of God's plan. If he hadn't stepped out into the unknown, he wouldn't have reached the fullness of his destiny. When you have the boldness to go out, not knowing all the details, your life will be more rewarding and more fulfilling than you ever imagined.

Be Like Esther

There was a young Jewish girl in the Scripture named Esther. She was an orphan, didn't come from an influential family, and was living in a foreign country. But God raised her up to become the queen, and now she was living in the palace. There was a powerful official who was able to pass a law that all the Jewish people be killed. Esther's uncle Mordecai told her of the decree and said that she had to go in and plead with the king for their people. In those days, if you approached the king without his holding up his golden rod first, you would be killed. She said, "Mordecai, I can't just go in there. What if he doesn't hold it up? That will be the end of me." God was asking her to step into the unknown, but the what-ifs started coming. "What if the king is offended, gets upset, and doesn't hold it up? I'll be dead." She was about to talk herself out of it. But Mordecai said, "Esther, if you keep silent, deliverance for the Jews will come from someone else, but you and your family will perish. Who knows but that you have come to the kingdom for such a time as this?" God was saying, "Esther, if you don't do it, I'll find somebody else. But the problem is that you're going to miss your destiny." This opportunity wasn't going to come again. This was her chance to make her mark. It was now or never. I love what Esther did. She rose up and said, "I will go before the king, which is against the law; and if I perish, I perish! But I will not let this moment pass." She stepped up, and not only did God give her favor with the king, but she saved her people and became one of the heroes of faith.

Like Esther, we all have opportunities that are not going to come our way again. When my father died and I had to make that choice to step up or play it safe, that was one of those now-or-never moments. When they come your way, don't shrink back, don't let

> *Like Esther, we all have opportunities that are not going to come our way again.*

fear talk you out of it, and don't let the what-ifs keep you in your boat. Do as Esther did. Be bold, be courageous, and step into the unknown. You may not have all the details, and you may not see how it's going to work out, but along the way through the darkness you'll see miracles. If you'll do this, I believe you're about to step into a new level of favor, a new level of influence, a new level of anointing. You're going to rise higher, accomplish your dreams, and reach the fullness of your destiny.

CHAPTER SIXTEEN

I'm Still Standing

The Scripture says, "Rain falls on the just and on the unjust." No matter how good a person you are, there's going to be some rain in your life. Being a person of faith doesn't exempt you from difficulties. Jesus told a parable about a wise man who built his house on a rock. This man honored God. Another man foolishly built his house on the sand. He didn't honor God. Then the rain descended, the floods came, and the winds blew and beat on the houses. What's interesting is that the same storm came to both people, the just and the unjust. If the story stopped there, you'd think that it doesn't make a difference whether we honor God or not. "The same thing happens to me that happens to everyone else. I built my house on the rock, and yet I'm in this storm. I got a bad medical report, my child is off course, and I lost my biggest client." But that's not the end of the story. If you judge it too soon, it will seem as though faith doesn't make a difference.

Jesus went on to tell that after the storm was over, the house built on the rock was still standing. The house built on the sand collapsed and was completely ruined. The difference is that when you honor God, the storms may come, but you have a promise that the others don't have—when it's all said and done, you'll still be standing. In tough times you have to remind yourself, "This is not the end. My house is built on the rock. The enemy doesn't have the final say; God does, and He says that when it's all over, I'll still be standing." You may get knocked down, but you won't get knocked out. You may suffer a setback and have to go through some dark, stormy times, but don't get discouraged or bitter—that's just a part of life. It rains on everybody. If you'll stay in faith, you have God's promise that when the smoke clears, when the dust settles, you won't be the victim, you'll be the victor. You'll still be standing.

> *The storms may come, but you have a promise that the others don't have—when it's all said and done, you'll still be standing.*

All of us can look back and see things that should have defeated us. You may have gone through a divorce or a breakup that could have given you a nervous breakdown, but look at you—you're still standing, still happy, restored, and whole. That's the goodness of God. That addiction, all that partying, should have killed you, but because of your praying mother, you're still standing—clean, sober, and free. The medical report said you were done, that sickness would end your life, but God said, "I have another report. It's not over. You're still standing." Maybe you lost a loved one and didn't think you could go on, believing your best days were over; but God breathed new life into you, lifted you out of the pit, put a new song in your heart, and here you are still standing. You've been through some difficult, dark places, but you've also seen the goodness of God. You've seen Him lift you, restore you, heal you, and protect you. When you have this history with God, and you remember what He's done, you don't get discouraged by every difficulty, you don't get upset when people talk negatively about you, and you don't fall apart when you have a disappointment. You know that God brought you through the darkness in the past, and He'll bring you through in the future.

You Have Bounce-Back

About a year after I took over as pastor from my father, I heard that a couple who had been longtime members was going to leave the church. They didn't like the direction I was taking it in. I was young and doing my best, and the last thing I wanted was to lose any members, let alone longtime members. When I heard that, my first thought was, *Oh man, I can't believe this is happening.* I was tempted to get down and discouraged, but then something rose up in me. I thought to myself, *I made it through the death of my father. I went through my darkest hour and here I am, still standing. I can make it through their leaving. I made it through my mother's having terminal cancer. I made it through a three-and-half-year lawsuit to get this building. I made it through the critics who said that I couldn't minister. I made it through my own thoughts telling me that I wasn't qualified. If I can make it through all that, I can make it without that couple's being here.* I heard God saying right down in my heart, "Joel, don't worry. They may leave, but I'm not going to leave. When it's all said and done, just like all those other times, you'll still be standing."

If you are going through a difficult time, you need to look back and remember what God has done. He made a way when you didn't see a way, and He opened doors that you could never have opened. He put you at the right place at the right time. He vindicated and restored you. He did it for you in the past, and He'll do it for you again. Your house is built on the rock. You have the promise that no matter what comes your way, when the storm is over, when the trouble passes, when the opposition ceases, one thing you can count on is that you'll still be standing. You have the DNA of Almighty God. You may get knocked down, you may have a setback, but you're not going to stay down. There's something in your DNA that says, "Get back up again. That's not where you belong. You're a child of the Most High God."

We had a hurricane in Houston a few years ago. All kinds of trees were blown down. Huge oaks that were four or five feet around and looked as sturdy as can be were no match for winds of one hundred miles per hour. Pine trees over a hundred feet tall were lying in yard after yard. Big trees, small trees, oaks, pines, elms, and magnolias— none of them could withstand the hurricane-force winds. There was only one type of tree that I noticed wasn't blown down—the palm tree. It's because God designed the palm tree to withstand the storms. Unlike most other trees, the palm tree is able to bend so it will not break. A certain kind of palm can bend over until the top is almost touching the ground. During a hurricane, it may stay all bent over for three or four hours. It looks as though it's done, as though it's finished. I can imagine that hurricane huffing and puffing, thinking, *I may not be able to blow you down like I can the oaks and the pines, but at least I can cause you to be all bent over. At least I can keep you from ever standing up tall again.* That hurricane keeps blowing and blowing, thinking that it's winning the battle, and after a few hours it runs out of strength and the wind subsides. And you know what happens next? The palm tree stands right back up as it did before. Why is that? God put bounce-back in the palm tree. It may get pushed over, but that's only temporary. It's just a matter of time before the palm tree rises up again.

Psalm 92 says, "The righteous will flourish like a palm tree." It could have said that we'd flourish like an oak tree and that we'd have big, strong, wide branches. It could have said that we'd flourish like a pine tree and be so tall and impressive that we'd be seen for miles. The reason God said we'd flourish like a palm tree is that God knew we would go through difficult times. He knew things would try to

"I'm going to make you like a palm tree. I'm going to put bounce-back in your spirit."

push us down and keep us from our destiny, so He said, "I'm going to make you like a palm tree. I'm going to put bounce-back in your spirit. You may go through a dark period of loneliness, of loss, of disappointment. The rain will come, but don't get discouraged. It's only temporary. At some point the winds will subside, the storm will pass, and just as with that palm tree, the bounce-back put in you by your Creator is going to cause you to stand right back up. Don't believe the lies that it's permanent. Don't believe that you'll never get well, never overcome the addiction, or never get out of the legal situation. No, your house is built on the rock. You may be bent over right now, you may have some difficulties, but when the storm is over, you'll still be standing.

What's interesting is that when the palm tree is bent over during the hurricane, you would think that's damaging the tree and making it weaker, but research shows just the opposite. When it's being pushed and stretched by the strong winds, that's strengthening the root system and giving it new opportunities for growth. After the storm, when the palm tree straightens back up, it's actually stronger than it was before. When you come out of the storm, when you straighten back up, you're not going to be the same. You're going to be stronger, healthier, wiser, better off, and ready for new growth. God never brings you out the same. He makes the enemy pay for bringing the times of darkness and trouble. What's meant for your harm He's going to use to your advantage. It's not going to break you; it's going to strengthen you. You're not only going to still be standing; you're going to be standing stronger.

Better, Stronger, and More Blessed

I have a friend who's had cancer three times over the past ten years. A couple of times it looked as though he were done. I never once heard him complain, never saw him down. He knows that God has him in the palms of His hands. He knows that the number of his days, God will fulfill. He has his house built on the rock. Every time it looks as though it's over, like that bent-over palm tree, somehow he bounces back. When the cancer came back the third time, the doctors told him they were going to harvest his white blood cells before he was given the chemotherapy in two months. He asked how many cells they needed to help restore his immune system after the treatment. When they gave him a number, he said, "I'll give you twice what you need." Every day he thanked God that he was getting better, and he saw himself as healthy and whole. He went out and exercised, did everything he could. Two months later, he went back to the hospital, and the doctors said, "You kept your word. You gave us more than twice the number of white blood cells we were hoping for." Today he's cancer-free, having beaten it for the third time.

Like that palm tree, no matter how hard those winds blow, you cannot be uprooted, you cannot be toppled, you cannot be broken. Sickness doesn't determine your destiny; God does. He's the one who breathed life into you. If it's not your time to go, you're not going to go. God has the final say, and He said, "No weapon formed against you will prosper." He said, "Many are the afflictions of the righteous, but the Lord delivers us out of them all." He said, "A good man may fall seven times, but the Lord will raise him up." That's the bounce-back.

> *Like that palm tree, no matter how hard those winds blow, you cannot be uprooted, you cannot be toppled, you cannot be broken.*

Now you have to get in agreement with God. Don't have a weak, defeated mentality that says, "Why did this happen to me? I don't understand it." It happened because you're alive—it's just a part of life. It rains on all of us. The good news is, because you're the righteous, you have something in you that the unrighteous don't have. Like that palm tree, you have bounce-back on the inside. No matter how hard those winds blow, they cannot defeat you. If you'll stay in faith, you'll be able to say, as my friend says, "I'm still standing. Sickness knocked me down for a little while, but I came right back up." You'll be able to say, "I went through a slow season at work, had some bad breaks, but it didn't defeat me. I came out promoted and stronger. I'm still standing." You'll be able to say, "I went through a breakup. Somebody walked out on me and caused me heartache and pain. I didn't think I'd ever be happy again, but look what the Lord has done. He brought somebody better into my life."

I met a young couple who had moved to Houston from New Orleans. They lost everything during Hurricane Katrina. The house they had worked so hard for was totally ruined, as well as their furniture and car. They made it out with only the clothes on their backs. The husband's company had closed down, so he no longer had a job. A bus dropped them off at the Astrodome. When I first saw them, it was as though they were numb. Their whole world had fallen apart. I told them what I'm telling you. "You may be down right now, but that's temporary. You have bounce-back in your spirit. When it's all said and done, you'll still be standing, stronger, healthier, and better." Week after week, they kept coming to Lakewood, hearing about how we are victors and not victims, how God will pay us back for the unfair things, and how what's meant for our harm God will use to our advantage. A couple of years later, they brought pictures of the beautiful new house they had just bought. They'd had an older house in New Orleans, and they now have a brand-new one here. The man told how he had a better job, with better benefits. Their kids were in better schools. That's what happens when your house is built on the rock. It doesn't prevent difficulties. You may go through some storms, you may have some bad breaks, but there's bounce-back in your DNA. When it's all over, you'll still be standing—but better, stronger, and more blessed.

A Warrior Mentality

The Scripture says, "When the enemy comes in like a flood." That means you feel overwhelmed—you lost your house in a hurricane, you got a bad medical report, a relationship went sour, somebody cheated you in a business deal. What does God do when the enemy comes in like this? Does He sit back and say, "Too bad. I told you it was going to rain. I told you that you're going to have difficulties"? No, Scripture says, "When the enemy comes in like a flood, the Spirit of the Lord will raise up a barrier." In other words, the difficulties, the injustices, and the sicknesses get God's attention. He goes to work just as we do as parents when we see our child in trouble, perhaps because someone is mistreating them. Like us, He doesn't think twice about stopping what He's doing and going to help.

When our son, Jonathan, was about two years old, we were in the grocery store. I had walked down to the end of the aisle, and he had stayed by the cart. I could see him, but I was about forty feet away. As I was looking for something, he started pulling a few boxes of cereal off the bottom shelf. It was no big deal. I was going to pick the boxes up and put them back. But a lady who worked there came around the corner and was immediately very upset that he had made a mess. She nearly yelled with an angry tone, "Young man, you cannot take these boxes off the shelf! You need to keep your hands to yourself!" When I heard that, something rose up in me. I don't know if it was God or the devil. I'm nice, I'm kind, and I'll do anything for you, but if you mess with my children, I turn into the Incredible Hulk.

That's the way God is. When the enemy comes in like a flood, God steps up and says, "Hey, wait a minute! You're messing with the wrong person. That's My child. That's My son. That's My daughter. If you're going to mess with them, you have to first mess with Me. Who am I? I am the all-powerful Creator of the universe. When I said,

> *A warrior doesn't complain about opposition; a warrior loves a good fight. It fires him up.*

'Let there be light,' light burst forth at 186,000 miles per second." God looks at your enemies and says, "You want some of this? Go ahead and make My day!" In the tough dark times, you have to realize that you're not alone. The Most High God is fighting for you. He's got your back. He's brought you through in the past, and He's going to bring you through in the future. Now you have to do your part and get your fire back. You can't sit around in self-pity and think about what you lost, who hurt you, and how unfair it was. That's going to keep you down. Shake off that weak, defeated, *Why did this happen to me?* mentality and have a warrior mentality. A warrior doesn't complain about opposition; a warrior loves a good fight. It fires him up.

This is what David did when he went through a big disappointment. While he and his men were out protecting the borders of Israel, doing the right thing, fulfilling his purpose, bandits came in and attacked his home city of Ziklag. They burned down the houses, stole the people's belongings, and took captive all the women and children. When David and his six hundred men returned and saw the smoke and realized what had happened, they sat down among the ashes and wept until they could weep no more. It was the worst day of their lives, and it was David's greatest defeat. He was deeply distressed, and there was talk among his men of stoning him. It looked as though it was over, and it would have stayed that way if it had not been for David. He did something that we all must do if we're going to see the bounce-back. Instead of his staying in the ashes, thinking about how badly life had treated him, the warrior spirit rose up on the inside. He said, "Wait a minute. I may be down and discouraged, and I've suffered my worst loss, but this is not the end of the story. I am the righteous. I have bounce-back in my spirit. My house is built on the rock. I have a promise that when it's all over, I'll still be standing." He started encouraging himself in the Lord, reminding himself of who he was and Whose he was. He told his men, "Get up, dry your tears, and shake off the discouragement. We're going to go get what belongs to us." They went out and not only attacked and defeated their enemies, but got all their possessions back, as well as their wives and children.

The Scripture says that they "recovered all." David's greatest defeat turned into his greatest victory.

We all face unfair situations. We may find ourselves in dark places, such as David experienced, that look as though you're going to be buried. But if you'll have this warrior mentality, if you'll stir your faith up and go after what belongs to you, the enemy won't have the last laugh; you will. He may hit you with his best shot, but his best will never be enough. You have bounceback in your spirit. The forces that are for you are greater than the forces that are against you. Like David,

> *Like David, you may be down for a season, and it may pour rain and flood, but because your house is built on the rock, because you have this warrior mentality, when it's all said and done, you'll still be standing.*

you may be down for a season, and it may pour rain and flood, but because your house is built on the rock, because you have this warrior mentality, when it's all said and done, you'll still be standing.

Standing as the Victor

One time I was lifting weights at home, lying on a bench, doing the bench press. I had a barbell with free weights and was doing my last set of five repetitions. By my standards I had a lot of weight on the barbell, almost twice my weight. I did one lift, two, three, and everything was fine, just like normal; but on the fourth lift, I really struggled, could barely get it up. I thought, *Okay, I'm going to try five. This is going to be tough!* I got my fifth lift up about halfway and got stuck. I pushed and pushed and pushed, gave it everything I had, but it wouldn't budge. I couldn't do it! Then I began to set the barbell down on the safety rails so I could get out from under it. The only problem was that my son, Jonathan, had moved the rails down lower when he was working out, and I'd forgotten to check them. Now I had all the weight on my chest, and I was totally out of energy. I couldn't shake the weights off to one side because there were clamps on the ends of the barbell. I've rolled the barbell down to my stomach before when I've gotten stuck, but I couldn't do it with this heavy weight. My first thought was, *How long can I hold this off my chest before it crushes me?* I thought probably about a minute or two. My next thought was, *You've already wasted thirty seconds.*

As I was stuck there, not knowing what to do, something rose up in me and said, "Joel, you are not going to let this weight crush you. You are not going to let your family come in here and find you squashed. This is not the end of your story. You're too young to die. You have too much in you to die." I pushed on the right side with all my might. The left side hit the safety rail way down low, and I scooted over about an inch. I rested for a few seconds, then pushed on that right side again and scooted another inch. Then another inch, and I finally got my shoulder off the bench and then my chest. At one point I was able fall off the bench and let the safety rail catch the right side.

Here's my point. When you're in a tough time, you can't sit around and think about the bad break and how unfair it was. "I can't believe I have this sickness." "I can't believe they left me." "I can't believe I'm having to start all over." You can either let that sickness, that breakup, or that disappointment crush you and finish you off under the weight of it, or you can have a warrior spirit and do what you have to do to beat it. Push, scoot, squirm, stretch, wiggle, refocus, get your second wind, and beat it! When I got up off the ground, my chest was a little red and my back was a little scraped, but I thought, *At least I'm still alive.* I looked at those weights and said, "You didn't get the best of me. I'm still standing."

The Scripture says, "You have armed me with strength for the battle." I've found that the more difficult the battle, the more strength you'll have.

Your strength will always match what you're up against. When I think about how I got out from under that heavy barbell, I don't know how I did it. I was totally winded and had exhausted all my strength trying to finish the fifth rep. I could have said, "God, just take this off me. It's going to kill me." God said, "Push again and watch what will happen." I pushed and discovered strength that I hadn't known I had. Are you letting something defeat you because you don't think you have the strength to endure, the strength to overcome, the strength to deal with that sickness, that financial difficulty? If you'll have a warrior spirit and start doing what you can, God will help you do what you can't.

I saw a story on television news about a man who came up to a car that had crashed on the freeway. There was a person trapped inside, and the car had caught on fire. The man, who was about my size, grabbed the top of the door frame and somehow ripped the door away from the car so the trapped person could get out. They showed a picture of the steel frame, which looked like something a movie superhero had bent. They asked the man how he'd

> *When you do what you have to do, you'll discover strength that you didn't know you had.*

done it. He said, "I don't know. I just pulled as hard as I could." When you do what you have to do, you'll discover strength that you didn't know you had.

You are not weak or defeated; you are a warrior. You have resurrection power on the inside. You may be down right now, those winds are blowing, but like that bent-over palm tree, you're not going to stay down. You're about to come back up again, better off—stronger, healthier, and promoted. This is a new day. Things are changing in your favor. God has done it in the past, and He's going to do it in the future. You need to get ready, there's a bounce-back coming. You're going to bounce back from sickness, bounce back from depression, bounce back from bad breaks, bounce back from loss. Those winds can't uproot or topple you. The enemy doesn't have the final say; God does. He says that because your house is built on the rock, when it's all said and done, when the dark storm passes and the floods and winds subside, you'll still be standing, not the victim but the victor!

CHAPTER SEVENTEEN

Remember Your Dream

All of us have things we're believing for, things we want to accomplish. Deep down we feel them very strongly. We know they're a part of our destiny, but then we hit some setbacks. We didn't get the promotion, the relationship didn't work out, or the medical report wasn't good. Life has a way of pushing our dreams down. They can become buried under discouragement, buried under past mistakes. There are dreams buried under rejection, divorce, failure, and negative voices. It's easy to settle for mediocrity when we have all this potential buried inside. But just because you gave up doesn't mean God gave up. Your dream may be buried in a dark place, but the good news is, it's still alive. It's not too late to see it come to pass. We've all been through disappointments and bad breaks as life happens to us. But instead of remembering the hurts, the failures, and what didn't work out, the key to reaching your destiny is to remember your dream. Remember what God promised you. Remember what He whispered to you in the middle of the night.

The Scripture calls these dreams "the secret petitions of your heart." They're the things you may not have told anybody else about. They may seem impossible. Every voice tells you they're not going to happen. You've pushed them down, but God is saying, "What I've promised you, I'm still going to do. I spoke it and put it in your heart. It may not have happened yet, but I am true to My word. It's on the way." If you'll start believing again, get your passion back, stir your faith up, God is going to resurrect what you thought was dead. You may have tried and failed, and it was so long ago, but dreams that you've given up on are going to suddenly come back to life. Problems that looked permanent are going to suddenly turn around. What should have taken years to restore, God is going to give you in a fraction of the time. He has the final say. He hasn't changed His mind.

Don't let circumstances talk you out of it. You may not understand why something happened—

> *Dreams that you've given up on are going to suddenly come back to life.*

why a person walked away, why you came down with that illness, why the business didn't make it. You were doing the right thing, but the wrong thing happened. It's all a part of the process. Every unfair situation, every delay, and every closed door is not a setback; it's a setup for God to get you to where He wants you to be. It may be taking a long time, and you may not see how it can happen, but all it takes is one touch of God's favor.

Why are you remembering the hurt, the disappointment, and the times it didn't work out? Turn it around and start remembering your dream. What has God put in your heart? What did you used to be excited about? Why do you think it's too late, it's too big, it's not possible? Why don't you think you can write the book, start the business, see the relationship restored, or finish school? Get your passion back. You haven't missed your opportunity or had too many bad breaks. You're not lacking, and you didn't get shortchanged.

Get Your Shovel Out

When God breathed His life into you, He put in you everything you need to fulfill your destiny. People can't stop you, and neither can bad breaks, disappointments, or loss. The Most High God is on your side. You have royal blood flowing through your veins. You have seeds of greatness. There are dreams in you so big that you can't accomplish them on your own. It's going to take you connecting with your Creator, believing that you're a person of destiny, knowing that God is directing your steps. We all face challenges, but we don't have to get discouraged. God controls the whole universe. He won't allow anything to happen unless He has a way to bring good out of it. But you have to stir up your gift. The enemy would love for you to keep your dream buried and wants to convince you that it's never going to happen, that it's too late. Don't believe those lies. You can still accomplish your dreams. You can still become all you were created to be. Every time you remember your dream, every time you say, "Lord, thank You for bringing it to pass," you're removing some dirt. You're digging it out.

Maybe you've been dealing with an illness for a long time. Early on you believed you would get well, but now it's been years. You've just learned to live with it. What's happened is that your healing, your breakthrough, your freedom have gotten buried. They're still in you; they're still alive. If you'll get your fire back, start believing again, God can bring it to pass. When you're thinking, *It will never happen. I've had so many negative reports,* that's putting more dirt on it. That's burying it deeper. Why don't you get your shovel out and start removing the dirt? How do you do that? Say, "Lord, thank You that You're restoring health to me. Thank You that I'm free from this addiction, free from this depression. Thank You that my best days are still in front of me." If you'll keep talking like that, the dream that's been buried will come back to life. That's what allows God to do great things. He's moved by our faith. He's not moved by our doubts, by our discouragement, or by our complaining.

"But Joel, I'll never meet the right person. I've been hurt too many times." You're remembering the wrong thing. As long as you dwell on the hurt, you're going to get stuck. Start remembering the dream. "Lord, You said that You would bring the perfect person into my life. I want to thank You for a divine connection, somebody better than I ever imagined." Stop saying, "I could never accomplish my goal. I'll never get this promotion. I don't have the talent. I've tried, but I always get passed over." That's burying the dream, putting more dirt on it. You need to get a shovel and start digging that

> *As long as you dwell on the hurt, you're going to get stuck. Start remembering the dream.*

dream out. You may have been doing this for so long that you need a backhoe. You need some heavy equipment because it's buried way down deep in the darkness. You can dig it up and bring it to life. It starts in your thinking, in what you're believing, and in what you're saying. No more "It's never going to happen. I'm never going to have a nice house or get my degree." No, you have to say, "I'm surrounded by God's favor. Blessings are chasing me down. Because I delight myself in the Lord, He will give me the desires of my heart." Whatever God has put on the inside, no matter how long it's been, no matter how impossible it looks, I'm asking you to stir it up. You have to get in agreement with God. He's the giver of all dreams. He's the one who put that desire in you. You may need to get alone, be quiet, and search your heart. Say to Him, "God, anything that I've pushed down, anything that I've given up on, show me what it is. God, don't let me die with any dreams still buried."

"Give Me This Mountain"

This is what Caleb did. When he and Joshua were young men, they were sent to spy out the Promised Land. They came back and told Moses and all the people of Israel, "We are well able to take the land. Let us go in at once." But the other ten spies said just the opposite, speaking only of great fortified cities and giants who made them feel like grasshoppers. The Israelites, some two million people, were terrified by the negative report, and even though they were camped next door to the Promised Land, they turned around, and that group of people never went in. I can imagine Caleb was discouraged. He knew they were supposed to go in. God put that dream in his heart, but it didn't happen. It looked as though the other people had kept him from his destiny. That could have been the end of Caleb's story, which would have been too bad for him because he'd had some unfair breaks. His dream had gotten buried, but it wasn't his fault. Most people would have given up and settled where they were, but not Caleb. The true mark of a champion is that even when some dirt gets thrown on a dream, instead of letting it get buried, they keep shaking it off. They keep looking for new ways to move forward, believing for new opportunities.

Forty years later, when Caleb was eighty-five years old, he could still feel this dream stirring inside. He wasn't sitting around feeling sorry for himself, saying, "I really tried. If only those other people had done what was right. If only I hadn't had those bad breaks. I was so close. I guess it wasn't meant to be." At eighty-five Caleb went back to that same mountain where the giants still lived, the same place where the others refused to go, and he said, "God, give me this mountain." What's significant is that there were three giants living on that mountain—three Goliaths. There were many other mountains with less opposition that would have been much easier to conquer. I can hear a friend say, "Come on, Caleb, you're eighty-five. Here, take this easy mountain instead." He would have said, "No, thanks. I'm not going to settle for mediocrity when God has placed greatness in me. I want that mountain. That's the dream that's been burning in me for all these years." He stirred it up. Forty years after the dream was given, he went and conquered the mountain that God had promised him. The dream came to pass.

Have you allowed any dreams to get buried in you? At one time you thought you could do something great—perhaps you thought you could lead a company or break an addiction—but that was a long time ago. You had some bad breaks that weren't your fault. You have a good excuse to settle; nobody would blame you if you did. But God sent me to light a fire inside you. That dream is still alive. You may have tried to make it happen a year ago, or five years ago, or forty years ago, but it didn't work out. Nobody helped you, and nobody encouraged you. God is saying to you what he said to Caleb: "Go back and try again. This is your time. This is your moment. Your destiny is calling out to you." You have to be like Caleb. You can't have a give-up spirit and take the easy way out. Don't settle for less than your dream and refuse to enter the struggle. Your destiny is at stake! If you don't stir up your gifts, you could miss what you were created to be. You may have been knocked down, but you have to get back up and say, "God, give me that same mountain. I don't want a substitute. I don't want second best. I don't want less-than. God, I'm going after what You put in my heart." When you remember the dream, God will help you accomplish what you didn't accomplish early on. You can still become all you were created to be.

I saw a report about a man who had been raised in a very dysfunctional environment. His dad was not a part of his life, and his mother was seldom around. He grew up in low-income government housing. From the time he was a little boy, he had a desire to be a writer. He went to school, but there was no structure in his life; there was nobody guiding him. At fifteen he dropped out of school, having never learned how to read or write. He was so embarrassed that he started drinking, trying to numb the pain. For thirty-five years all he did was hang out on the street and drink with his buddies. But one day something rose up in him like a fire. He told his buddies that he'd had enough, he was fed up with living that way, and that was going to be the last drink they'd ever see him take. They laughed and thought he was joking. But that day was a turning point. He was set free from alcohol and never touched it again. At fifty-one years old he went back to school and learned how to read and write and earned his diploma. He was so proud. Then he started writing poetry. He was a very gifted, eloquent writer. That dream had been buried deep under dysfunction, under bad breaks, and under addictions, but it was still alive. He entered a writing contest and won third place. He kept getting better, improving his craft, then entered a national contest and won the grand prize, first place. At seventy-five years old, he continues to write and inspire people, letting them know that it's never too late to accomplish their dreams.

What you gave up on, God didn't give up on. What you wanted to do earlier in life didn't go away just because it didn't work. It's still in you. When the prophet Jeremiah was so discouraged by being persecuted and mocked for speaking God's word that you thought he was going to quit, he suddenly said, "But Your word, O Lord, is like a burning fire shut up in my bones." I believe there are some dreams shut up in you that are like a fire. You're going to feel your destiny calling you. You tried to get away from it when it didn't work out the first time—the loan didn't go through,

> *I believe there are some dreams shut up in you that are like a fire. You're going to feel your destiny calling you.*

you didn't get the part, the report didn't come back good. That's okay. This is a new day. What God started, He's going to finish. You may have missed some opportunities, but God knows how to make up for lost time. He's going to give you another chance. He says in the book of Joel, "I will restore to you the years." You may have lost years because other people put you at a disadvantage or because of your own choices, but God knows how to make up for it. He can still get you to where you're supposed to be.

Be a Dreamer

I previously shared that God gave Joseph a dream that one day his parents and his brothers would bow down before him. Joseph should have used more wisdom and not told them about his dream.

Certain things you should keep to yourself. Some people can't handle what God has put in you. They won't celebrate you; rather, like Joseph's brothers, they'll get jealous of you and start finding fault. One day Joseph went to see his ten brothers, who were away feeding their father's flock. When he walked up, one of them said sarcastically, "Here comes the dreamer." In the past the brothers had been upset because Joseph was their father's favorite son and because their father had given Joseph a special coat of many colors. But now they were even more upset because he'd had a dream. They were offended because he was determined to break out of the family mold, to do something greater than what they had done, to leave his mark. They would have been fine if he were content to be average, to accept the status quo. But when you stir up what God has put in you, when you believe that you have seeds of greatness, let me warn you that not everybody will celebrate you.

When you have a dream, you're going to have some detractors. When you believe that you can overcome an illness, pay off your house, start a business, or be successful in spite of past mistakes, some people will become jealous and try to make you look bad or try to talk you out of it. "Do you really think you'll get that promotion? You don't have the experience." "Do you really think you'll meet the right person? It didn't work out the last three times you tried. You're getting kind of old." Let that go in one ear and out the other. The critics, the naysayers, and the haters don't control your destiny. God does. They can't keep you from your dreams. They may do something that puts you at a disadvantage, but God knows how to take what was meant for your harm and use it to promote you.

Joseph's own brothers tried to push his dream down. I say this respectfully, but sometimes your relatives won't celebrate you. Sometimes the people closest to you will be the least supportive. Here's the key: don't get distracted with fighting battles that don't matter, trying to prove to

> *Successful people, people who have and pursue a dream, don't waste their time looking at what everybody else is doing.*

them who you are, trying to convince them to believe in you. You don't need their approval. You have Almighty God's approval. Let them go. The haters are going to hate. What stirs them up is the fact that you're moving forward, pursuing your destiny. They want you to keep your dream buried in a dark place so you don't rise higher and make them look bad. They don't realize God has put dreams in them as well. If they would stir their dreams up, they wouldn't be jealous. They could rise higher and fulfill their own purposes. Successful people, people who have and pursue a dream, don't waste their time looking at what everybody else is doing. They're too busy focusing on what God has put in their hearts.

The enemy targets people who have a dream. He'll use opposition, delays, discouragement, jealousy, and everything else he can to try to convince you to bury that dream. If you're going to reach your full potential, you have to make up your mind that you are in it for the long haul. You're not going to let people talk you out of it. You're not going to let circumstances discourage you, or let delays cause you to give up, or let critical people get you distracted. You stay focused on your goal. Here's the key: you wouldn't have that opposition if you didn't have something great in you. If that dream weren't alive and on track, right on schedule to come to pass, you wouldn't have so many things coming against you. But when the enemy looks at you, he says, "Oh no, here comes another dreamer. Here comes another person full of faith, believing they have seeds of greatness, not moved by their circumstances, not depressed because they had a bad break, not giving up because it's taking a long time. They're a dreamer. They know that they have the favor of God. They know that nothing is impossible because they believe. They know that God can make a way when they don't see a way."

Remember the Promise

When you're a dreamer, you're dangerous to the enemy. He knows that you're headed for new levels. He knows that you're going to set a new standard for your family. He knows that you're coming into abundance, into overflow. And he knows that there's nothing he can do to stop you. The forces that are for you are greater than the forces that are against you. But he'll work overtime to try to convince you to settle where you are. You have to remember this principle: when negative things happen, they cannot stop your destiny; they are a sign that you're on the way to your destiny. Those bad breaks did not cancel your dreams; it's all a part of the process. The delay, the people who did you wrong, or the time it didn't work out is just another step on the way to your destiny.

After thirteen years of bad breaks and disappointments, Joseph interpreted a dream for the Pharaoh, who immediately made Joseph one of the most influential men of his day. Years later, there was a great famine in the land. People were in distress, trying to survive. Joseph's brothers, the same ones who'd thrown him into a pit and sold him into slavery, showed up at the palace looking to purchase food. Joseph was in charge of the food supply, and they were standing in front of him but didn't recognize him. You can imagine it was very dramatic for Joseph. These were the brothers who'd betrayed him and caused him so many years of heartache and pain. You would think that Joseph would be bitter, angry, and vindictive. This was his chance to pay them back, and he had the power to do it. But the Scripture says, "When Joseph saw his brothers, he remembered his dream." He didn't remember the hurt, or the betrayal, or the lonely nights, or the times he'd been confused. As they bowed down before him, he remembered the promise that God had spoken to him. All those bad breaks he had suffered through, all that time when it looked as though he had missed his destiny—the whole time God was in control, directing his steps. It was all a part of the plan to get him to where he was supposed to be. It was meant for his harm, but God turned it around and used it for his good.

When God gives you a dream, when He puts a promise in your heart, that doesn't mean it's going to come to pass without opposition, delays, and adversities. There will be things you don't understand. You'll have plenty of opportunities to get discouraged and frustrated, thinking it's never going to happen. *I must have heard God wrong. Nothing is going right.*

In the tough times you have to do as Joseph did and remember your dream.

In the tough times you have to do as Joseph did and remember your dream. God didn't bring you this far to leave you. You may not understand it, but God is in control. He's directing your steps. Now do your part, stay in faith, and keep a good attitude. Let God be your vindicator. Let God fight your battles. He has it all figured out. "Well, Joel, I'm in the pits. This is a dark place. I don't understand it." Don't worry, because a caravan is coming to move you to your next location. "A friend lied about me." "I went through a divorce." "I lost a loved one." Don't get bitter. It's just a detour on the way to your destiny. The palace is coming. The promise is still on track.

Just Passing Through

The Scripture speaks of "these light afflictions, which are but for a moment." When you face opposition and things don't go your way, recognize that it's not permanent. That's not your final destination. Quit worrying about things that are only temporary. As it was with Joseph, the pit—the betrayal, the injustice, the loneliness—is temporary. That's not your permanent home. It's a temporary stop. The psalmist wrote of "passing through the Valley of Weeping," not "settling in the Valley of Weeping," or "getting stuck in the Valley," or "building a house in the Valley." The Valley is temporary; you're passing through it. Now my challenge is to quit losing sleep over a temporary stop. Quit being stressed out over something that's only for a season; it's not permanent.

I was in my backyard one time and my grass looked dead. It was brown, worn out. I called a man who helps me with my landscaping and asked,

Your dream is not dead; it's just not in season. Your time is coming.

"What happened to my grass? Why did it die?" He said, "Joel, it's not dead. It's just not in season. It's fully alive, but it's dormant right now. In a few months it will be as green and full as can be." I was worried over something that was temporary. I thought that was the way it was always going to be. Once I realized that it was normal, I never worried about it again. When I saw that brown grass, I thought, *It's just a matter of time before it's back to green.* Are you worrying about things that are only temporary?

Are you letting something steal your joy because you think that it's over, that it's never going to work out? Your dream is not dead; it's just not in season. Your time is coming. The right people, the right opportunities, the healing, the vindication, the restoration are headed your way. The Scripture says "these light afflictions, which are but for a moment," and goes on to say, "They are working in us an eternal weight of glory." The affliction is temporary, but the glory is permanent.

Stir up what's on the inside. You may have a dream that you've buried and given up on. You need to get your shovel out and start thanking God that it's coming to pass. Maybe you're on a detour right now, going through something you don't understand. Don't get discouraged. You're just passing through. It's easy to remember the hurt and the disappointment. I'm asking you to remember the dream, remember the promise. If you do this, I believe that dreams you've buried will come back to life. Promises that you've given up on will be resurrected. As He did with Joseph, God is going to turn every stumbling block into a stepping-stone. You will rise higher, accomplish your goals, and become everything you were created to be.

CHAPTER EIGHTEEN

An Expected End

I was in the home of a well-known actor who not only stars in major movies but also writes them. We walked into a room with a large glass wall that overlooks his property. It seemed a bit strange that there were probably a hundred and fifty index cards stuck to the glass wall. He explained that he was writing a movie and that each card represented a different scene. He studies them and moves them around, adding a scene here and taking away a scene there. He explained that to make a good movie you have to have highs and lows, conflicts and victories, good and bad characters, twists and turns. While I found it very fascinating, it seemed so complicated, so confusing. I asked him, "How do you know where to start?" He said, "Oh, that's the easy part. You always start with your final scene. You have to establish how you want the movie to end. Once you establish the ending, you work backward and fill in all the details." He added, "In fact, you don't necessarily shoot the movie scenes in sequence. A lot of times you shoot the final scene first, and then shoot the rest of the movie."

This is what God has done for each one of us. The prophet Isaiah said, "God declares the end from the beginning." When God planned out your life, He started with your final scene. He started with where He wants you to end up, and then He worked backward. Here's the beauty of it. Jeremiah 29 says, "God's plans for you are for good and not for evil, to give you an expected end." Your end has already been established. Your final scene has already been shot. The good news is that you don't end in defeat, in failure, in disappointment, or in heartache. You end in victory, as more than a conqueror, as the head and not the tail, fulfilling your destiny. When you understand that your end has been established, you won't go through life upset because of a disappointment, frustrated because a dream hasn't

> *When you understand that your end has been established, you won't go through life upset because of a disappointment, frustrated because a dream hasn't come to pass, or bitter because of a loss.*

come to pass, or bitter because of a loss. You'll stay in peace, knowing that in the end, it's all going to work to your advantage.

But here's the key: as in a movie, there will be twists and turns. There will be times when you think, *I know I'm supposed to be going that way, but I'm headed just the opposite way. My goal is to get over there, so why am I facing the other direction?* There will be scenes in your life that on their own don't make sense. If you stopped right there at the divorce, the sickness, or the loss, it would look as though things didn't work out. It would look as though they got the best of you. But what you don't realize is that's not your final scene. As long as you have breath, your movie is still in development. You may be in a difficult scene right now, something you don't understand—a negative medical report, a setback in your finances—and it may look as though a dream has died. You have to remind yourself that that's not how your story ends. You have an expected end. The Creator of the universe, the Most High God, has already planned it for good and not harm. If you'll keep moving forward, there's going to be another twist coming, but this time it will be a good break, a promotion, a restoration, a healing. God knows how to weave it all together. He's already established the end.

Your Final Scene Has Been Shot

We see this principle with Joseph. God destined him to rule a nation, to become a leader in Egypt so he could help his family and the world in a time of widespread famine. That was the end. It was established. Joseph started off well. But his story took an unusually dark twist. His brothers were jealous of him, and they sold him into slavery. He could have thought, *I must not have heard God right. He gave me a dream that my family would bow down to me, but it sure didn't work out.* Joseph understood this principle. He knew that was just one scene. He knew the end had been set, so he just kept being his best. He was lied about and put in prison for something that he hadn't done. That was another strange twist that made it look as though he were being moved away from his destiny. This is the real test of faith. Will you keep a good attitude when you're doing the right thing but the wrong thing is happening? Will you be your best when you're not getting the credit you deserve? Will you stay passionate about life when the door closes, you don't get the promotion, or the medical report isn't good, and you feel as though you're going the wrong way?

This is where Joseph excelled. When he was falsely imprisoned, he didn't fall apart and become bitter. He just kept doing the right thing. If Joseph were here today, he would say, "Don't get discouraged by the detours, the strange twists, and the dark scenes you don't understand. They are all a vital part of your movie. They may not make sense on their own, but God knows how to weave it all together, and in the end you'll come out fulfilling your purpose, seeing what He promised."

This is where many people get frustrated and soured on life. "Joel, if God is good, why did I have this bad break?" "Why did I get laid off?" "Why did my relationship not make it?" We may never understand the whys, but I can tell you this: God wouldn't have allowed it if it weren't going to somehow work for your good. Nothing that's happened to you can keep you from your destiny. The only thing that can stop you is you. If you get negative and bitter and lose your passion, that's going to keep you from God's best. You may have had unfair things happen to you, but I've learned that the depth of your pain is an indication

> *Nothing that's happened to you can keep you from your destiny. The only thing that can stop you is you.*

of the height of your future. When construction workers are going to build a big high-rise, they have to first dig down many stories to build the foundation. The taller the building, the deeper the foundation. When you go through difficulties and unfair situations, it may be uncomfortable, you may not like it, but God is getting you prepared to be taken higher than you ever imagined. It may look as though something is there to defeat you, but God is going to use it to increase you. No bad break can stop you. All the forces of darkness cannot hold you down. God has an expected end for you; He's already established it.

But along the way not everything is going to make sense. This is where faith comes in. You have to trust that even in the scenes that you don't understand, in the twists of life, God knows what He's doing. As was true of Joseph, you know that God promised you one thing—influence, leadership, new levels—but that everything that's happening indicates just the opposite—defeat, betrayal, insignificance. That's when you have to dig your heels in and say, "God, I don't understand it, but I trust in You. I believe that Your plans for me are for good. I believe that You've already set my end and shot my final scene. I believe that I will fulfill my purpose and become who You created me to be."

If All Is Not Well, It's Not the End

I've heard it said that God always ends in "all is well." If all is not well, that means it's not the end. "Joel, it's not well in my finances. Business is slow, and I'm struggling." Don't get discouraged; it's not the end. That's just one scene. Favor is coming. Breakthroughs are coming. Abundance is coming. If it's not well in your health, don't settle there and think, *This is the way it's always going to be.* Another scene is coming. God promised that He will fulfill the number of your days. If it's not your time to go, you're not going to go. Maybe it's not well in a relationship—you went through a breakup, you're lonely, and you don't think you'll ever meet the right person. It's not the end. The person who left didn't stop God's plan. They didn't change His ending. They can't remake your movie. They don't have that kind of power. God has already established your ending. He's already lined up the person of your dreams, somebody better than you ever imagined. They're just a couple scenes away. It's just a matter of time before that person shows up.

The Scripture says, "For the Lord of hosts has purposed, and who can annul it?" This means that God has a purpose for your life. He's already planned out your days, lined up the different scenes, and established your ending. Then it asks, "Who can stop it?" God is saying, "I flung stars into space. I spoke worlds into existence. I'm the all-powerful Creator of the universe. Now, who can stop My plan for your life? Who can change your ending? People can't, unfair situations can't, tragedy can't. I have the final say." When you're on a detour, when you come to a dead end with something you don't understand, don't get upset or live frustrated. It's just one scene. When it all comes together, it's going to work out for your good. If Joseph hadn't been betrayed by his brothers, hadn't been sold into slavery, hadn't been falsely accused and put into prison, he wouldn't have made it to the throne. Those were all necessary scenes on the way to his established ending. What am I saying? What looks like a setback is really God setting you up to get you to the fullness of your destiny. You can go through life fighting everything that doesn't go your way, being worried, negative, and upset. Or you can stay in peace, knowing that God is directing your steps, even the detours, the dead ends, and the U-turns. It's all going to work to your advantage.

> *When it all comes together, as it did for Joseph, it's going to work out for your good.*

Sometimes when I'm traveling and not able to watch a ball game on television, I'll record it at home. The other day I recorded an important basketball game that I knew I was going to miss. The next week I sat down to watch it. I already knew the outcome. I had read the news reports and seen the highlights. The team I was pulling for had won. During the first quarter, my team played really badly, could hardly make a shot, and fell behind. I didn't get the least bit worried. I sat there calmly, enjoying the game. The star player got in foul trouble and had to sit on the bench, and we fell further behind. I didn't get uptight. The team came out in the second half and started off just as badly. They couldn't do anything right. Normally I would have been on edge, anxious, uptight, wondering what was going to happen. But because I knew the outcome, it totally changed my perspective. In fact, the further behind we fell, the more I thought, *This is going to be an exciting comeback. I can't wait to see what happens.* All the worry and anxiety had been taken away because of the expected end. I knew that we had won.

In life there are times when it looks as though our opponents—the sickness, the depression, the loss—are getting the best of us. We're falling behind. It's easy to look at the circumstances and get discouraged, thinking, *It's never going to work out. The odds are against me. The medical report says I'm not going to make it. I'll never accomplish my dreams.* Just as with that basketball game, you have to remind yourself that the end has been set. When it feels as though you're far behind, outnumbered, outsized, and outclassed, instead of being discouraged, have a new perspective. That means you're about to see a major comeback. At any moment things are going to shift in your favor. A good break, a healing, a promotion, or a restoration is coming. God has the final say. He said, "I always cause you to triumph." He didn't say "sometimes" or "most of the time." He's already shot your final scene. He's already lined up the victory parade.

A Flourishing Finish

A friend of mine was raised in a very dysfunctional home. His father died when he was four years old. His mother made a living by working the streets. When he was eleven years old, she left him on a street corner in a large city and said she would be back in a little while. Three days later, he was still on that street corner waiting for his mother. Confused, hungry, and afraid, he didn't know what to do. All the odds were against him. It didn't look as though he would ever amount to much. But when God breathed His life into him—and into you—He established the end first. He set your purpose. He gave you an assignment. He put in you everything you need to get to your destiny—the gifts, the talents, the confidence. He lined up the right people, the right breaks, and the solutions to problems.

How you start is not important. Don't let what you think is a disadvantage or a bad break cause you to say, "If I'd had a better childhood, if I had more support, if I didn't have this dysfunction, I could do something great." That's where you started, but that's not where you're going to finish. The begin-

> *The beginning doesn't determine your destiny. That's just one scene. What matters is the expected end.*

ning doesn't determine your destiny. That's just one scene. What matters is the expected end. The Creator of the universe has already destined you to leave your mark. He's already put seeds of greatness in you. God loves to take people who start with the odds against them and shine down His favor, give them breaks, promote them, increase them, and cause them to do extraordinary things.

That's what happened to my father. He came from a very poor family during the Great Depression. He had no money, little education, and no future to speak of. That's where he started, but that's not where he finished. His final scene, his established end, was pastoring a great church and having a ministry that touched the world. Don't let how you were raised, what you didn't get, or what looks like a disadvantage hold you back. God didn't breathe life into any person without giving them a destiny to fulfill. If you'll keep honoring God and being your best, you're moving toward the purpose God has designed for you. It's bigger than you imagine. It's more rewarding than you've ever dreamed.

The story of the eleven-year-old boy who was standing on the street corner did not end there. A man who traveled that way to work every day noticed him there for three days running. He stopped and asked if he needed help. The young boy told him that he had been abandoned and had nowhere to go. This man and his wife took him into their home and eventually adopted him. As he grew up, this young man had a desire to help other children in need. He told his pastor that he needed a van to pick up children in at-risk environments. Every week he would bring more and more needy children to Sunday school. It kept growing. Eventually, instead of a van he needed a school bus, and then another and another. Today this man has a ministry that reaches 150,000 children every week, giving them support and love, letting them know that they too can defy the odds and do something great in life. You may have had a rough start, but you're not going to have a rough finish. Somebody may have put you at a disadvantage, but they didn't change the expected end. What they did or didn't do cannot stop your destiny. Get rid of the excuses. Quit focusing on the bad breaks and the disappointments. God is in control of your life. He's directing your steps. He's already established the end.

The apostle Paul said in the book of Philippians, "God will bring us to a flourishing finish." He didn't say "to a defeated finish," "an unfair finish," "a lonely finish," or a "bankrupt finish." God has a victorious finish, an abundant finish, a fulfilled finish. When those thoughts tell you, "It's never going to work out. You have too many disadvantages. Your opponents are too big. You're too far behind, and you've made too many mistakes. This is as good as it gets," let those lies go in one ear and out the other. God is saying, "I'm going to take you further than you've imagined. I have explosive blessings that will catapult you ahead. I have favor that will thrust you into the fullness of your destiny. I'm going to bring out the seeds of greatness that I put in you." God has established the end, and He knows how to get you there. Now all through the day, just say, "Lord, I want to thank You that Your plans for me are for good. You're not limited by where I am right now. You've already shot my final scene. I may not understand everything along the way, and it may not have been fair, but I'm not going to live worried, upset, or discouraged. I know You're bringing me to a flourishing finish."

An *After This* Is Coming

In chapter two I wrote about the night season that Job endured. He went through some unusual twists and turns. Certain scenes didn't make sense. Nearly overnight his life went from being seemingly perfect to being shattered by great personal losses and covered in darkness. He could have given up on life and his faith. Even his wife told him, "Job, just curse God and die. You're done." Nothing like an encouraging spouse! In the midst of the difficulty, when everything was going wrong, when many people would have settled into being sour, bitter, and complaining, Job looked up to the heavens and said, "I know that my Redeemer lives." He was saying, in effect, "I know God is still on the throne. He's already established my end. He's already shot my final scene. If it's my time to go, I'm not going to go bitter or upset. Though He slay me, yet will I trust Him." When you can keep a good attitude when the bottom falls out, and when you can give God praise when life doesn't make sense, God will release you into a new level of your destiny. When you don't let the detours, the strange twists, and the things that you don't understand cause you to get sour, you pass the test and will see your established end.

At some point, of course, we're all going to die, but, like Job, I'm going to die in faith. I'm going to die believing. With my last breath, I'm going to be thanking God for the fullness of my destiny. We hear a lot about Job's trials, Job's suffering, and Job's loss. Yes, he went through a difficult season of darkness, but he didn't stay there. In the end he came out with twice what he'd had before. Scripture says that after this Job lived for another 140 blessed years.

Notice that after the difficulty, his life was not over, and he didn't end on a sour, defeated note. Just because you experience a twist, a detour, or a setback doesn't mean your life is over. God has an *after this* coming. When you go through tough times, you'll hear thoughts whispering, *You'll never be as happy*

> *You haven't laughed your best laugh, you haven't dreamed your best dream, you haven't danced your best dance, and you haven't sung your best song.*

again. You've seen your best days. This setback is going to be the end of you. Don't believe those lies. God is saying to you what He said to Job: "*After this*—the cancer, the layoff, the divorce, the legal problem—there is still a full life ahead of you." You haven't laughed your best laugh, you haven't dreamed your best dream, you haven't danced your best dance, and you haven't sung your best song. If you'll shake off the disappointment and get your passion back, God has an *after this* for you. He's not only going to bring you out, He's going to pay you back for that trouble. You're going to come out increased, promoted, and better than you were before.

When it was all over, Job said to God, "I'm convinced that nothing and no one can upset Your plans." He was saying that the expected end cannot be changed. God has already established it. The Scripture talks about how Satan had to ask for permission to test Job. The enemy can't do anything he wants; he has to get God's permission to touch you. God is not only in control of your life, He's in control of your enemies. You have nothing to worry about. He has a hedge of protection around you that cannot be penetrated. Nothing can snatch you out of God's hands.

Finish in Victory

When Jesus was about to be crucified, He told the people, "You can destroy this temple, but in three days I will raise it up." They thought He was talking about the building, but He was talking about Himself. He understood this principle that His end had been established. His final scene had already been shot. His final scene was not one of being betrayed and mistreated, hanging on a cross in great pain, or being buried in a tomb wrapped up in grave clothes. He knew that His final scene was that of being seated at the right hand of His Father, with all power, with the keys of death and hell. That's why Scripture says, "For the joy that was set before Him endured the cross, scorning its shame." In the tough times, the way to keep your joy is to keep looking ahead, knowing that the end has been set, knowing that you will have a flourishing finish, knowing that God always causes you to triumph.

The Scripture talks about how Jesus' body was placed in a borrowed tomb. He had no place of His own to be buried. One of His disciples came and put His body in a tomb that he owned. Before He was crucified, I

"I have an expected end that is set by My Father, and no enemy can change it."

can imagine Jesus asking that disciple if He could borrow the tomb. He was saying, "I don't need to buy it. This is not how My story ends. I don't end in defeat. This is temporary. I'll just be here a few days. I have an expected end that is set by My Father, and no enemy can change it. They can put Me in the ground, but they can't keep Me in the ground. I have an established end."

When we face difficulties, as Jesus did, our attitude should be, *I'm not staying here. This is temporary. I don't need to buy the tomb. This addiction is not how my story ends. This debt, this sickness, or this loss is just one scene. I know that another scene is coming—a scene of victory, a scene of promotion, a scene of breakthrough, a scene of restoration.*

Friend, your final scene has been shot. Now don't let the twists, the turns, and the dark places that don't make sense cause you to get discouraged. Keep moving forward. In the end it's all going to work to your advantage. As with that ball game I recorded, we know the final outcome. You don't have to worry or live upset. God has established your end. If you'll stay in faith and keep honoring God, He will get you to your throne as He did Joseph. He will pay you back for the trouble as He did Job. As He did for my friend who was abandoned, no matter how you start, God will cause you to finish in victory.

ACKNOWLEDGMENTS

In this book I offer many stories shared with me by friends, members of our congregation, and people I've met around the world. I appreciate and acknowledge their contributions and support. Some of those mentioned in the book are people I have not met personally, and in a few cases, we've changed the names to protect the privacy of individuals. I give honor to all those to whom honor is due. As the son of a church leader and a pastor myself, I've listened to countless sermons and presentations, so in some cases I can't remember the exact source of a story.

I am indebted to the amazing staff of Lakewood Church, the wonderful members of Lakewood who share their stories with me, and those around the world who generously support our ministry and make it possible to bring hope to a world in need. I am grateful to all of those who follow our services on television, the Internet, SiriusXM, and through the podcasts. You are all part of our Lakewood family.

I offer special thanks also to all the pastors across the country who are members of our Champions Network.

Once again, I am grateful for a wonderful team of professionals who helped me put this book together for you. Leading them is my Faith-Words/Hachette publisher, Rolf Zettersten, along with team members Patsy Jones, Billy Clark, and Hannah Phillips. I truly appreciate the editorial contributions of wordsmith Lance Wubbels.

I am grateful also to my literary agents Jan Miller Rich and Shannon Marven at Dupree Miller & Associates.

And last but not least, thanks to my wife, Victoria, and our children, Jonathan and Alexandra, who are my sources of daily inspiration, as well as our closest family members who serve as day-to-day leaders of our ministry, including my mother, Dodie; my brother, Paul, and his wife, Jennifer; my sister, Lisa, and her husband, Kevin; and my brother-in-law, Don, and his wife, Jackelyn.

We Want to Hear from You!

Each week, I close our international television broadcast by giving the audience an opportunity to make Jesus the Lord of their lives. I'd like to extend that same opportunity to you.

Are you at peace with God? A void exists in every person's heart that only God can fill. I'm not talking about joining a church or finding religion. I'm talking about finding life and peace and happiness. Would you pray with me today? Just say, "Lord Jesus, I repent of my sins. I ask You to come into my heart. I make You my Lord and Savior."

Friend, if you prayed that simple prayer, I believe you have been "born again." I encourage you to attend a good Bible-based church and keep God in first place in your life. For free information on how you can grow stronger in your spiritual life, please feel free to contact us.

Victoria and I love you, and we'll be praying for you. We're believing for God's best for you, that you will see your dreams come to pass. We'd love to hear from you!

To contact us, write to:

Joel and Victoria Osteen
P.O. Box 4600
Houston, TX 77210

Or you can reach us online at www.joelosteen.com.

Stay connected, be blessed.

From thoughtful articles to powerful blogs, podcasts and more, JoelOsteen.com is full of inspirations that will give you encouragement and confidence in your daily life.

Visit us today at JoelOsteen.com.